Cakes

TO CELEBRATE LOVE AND LIFE

Dedicated to Brian Hope Maximo Guy:

the next generation of our baking clan

CALLIE MARITZ AND MARI-LOUIS GUY

THANK YOU TO ...

Estee Maritz (mom) for love, everything and all things. Chris and Claudia for loving us (but then again, it's hard not to). Master baker, Riekie Booysens. Cobus van Niekerk for all the lovely props. Wallcoverings for awesome backdrops. Corne at Hertex for the gorgeous fabrics. Osiers for the use of beautiful props, bits and pieces. Simon at Earthcote for beautiful, massive backdrops for Chapter dividers. Nieleen for running after all of the above. Bettie for cleaning up every day's mess. Nicci at Aspen for fresh flowers and sticking around. Jackie Moore at Ingrid Moore for silk flowers. Christian Costa and Nancy Briggs for trends and ingredients. Helen Cubitt for lovely flowers. Dalene and all at Bakers Emporium, Cape Town's best baking supplier. Ryno Reyneke for pics (and mostly keeping his shirt on). Beverley Dodd for art direction and gorgeous layout. Linda VIP de Villiers for the opportunity. Petal for the inspiration for this book. Jeffrey Cheffrey for making it all look so easy. Dr Vosloo for being a mentor and a believer. Geraldine and all the staff at De Akker Guesthouse. Gifts for Guests for lovely treats packaging. Kobus Dippenaar for fab fabrics. Home etc and Mr Price Home for continued support in providing props.

Mari-Louis wants to thank Sonja 'Can't Bake, Won't Bake' Barlow (for blackmailing her name into print). Callie wants to thank Louis Broodryk (inspiration for life!).

> Please note that baking times may differ from oven to oven and for different heights above sea-level, so always check your cake towards the end of the baking time, either with a skewer (which should come out clean) or lightly press the centre of the cake by hand and feel for firmness. The best indicator for us is that when you can smell the cake in the kitchen, it is almost ready.

Published in 2009 by Struik Lifestyle

P.O. Box 1144 Cape Town 8000 South Africa
an imprint of Random House Struik (Pty) Ltd
Company Reg. No. 1966/003153/07
80 McKenzie Street Cape Town 8001 South Africa

www.randomstruik.co.za

www.imagesofafrica.co.za

IMAGES OF AFRICA
PHOTO LIBRARY

Over 40 000 unique African images available to
purchase from our image bank at
www.imagesofafrica.co.za

PUBLISHER: Linda de Villiers
MANAGING EDITOR: Cecilia Barfield
EDITOR: Joy Clack
DESIGNER: Beverley Dodd
PHOTOGRAPHER: Ryno
STYLISTS: Callie Maritz and Mari-Louis Guy
PROOFREADER: Tessa Kennedy
INDEXER: Joy Clack

Reproduction by Hirt & Carter Cape (Pty) Ltd
Printed and bound by Kyodo Nation Printing Services Co., Ltd

ISBN 978 1 77007 783 6

Contents

Cakes!

HEAVENLY, DELICIOUS, **DECADENT,** CRUMBLY, **SWEET CAKES!**

We love cake because it is meant as a celebration of love and life. We eat cake to celebrate a birth, a christening, a union between two people, a religious festival with family and loved ones or the end of a beautiful meal shared with good friends.

The secret ingredient in any cake is not found in many baking guides ... love!

All home-baked cakes are born from love. Love of baking, of creating, of giving. You bake a cake for someone because you love them, and it makes them – and you – feel special in the process.

We want you to get back into the kitchen and bake with love and passion. Soon you'll find that skill will follow. Whether you are an accomplished home-baker or breaking an egg into flour for the first time, we invite you on a journey through life with cake. We want you to experience that moment of feeling like an alchemist when you mix together some eggs, butter and flour, add some heat, and see this magically change into smiles on people's faces. That moment when you first realize that you can create a fantastic tasting cake, better than what you get from the shop, is indeed a revelation that we want all of you to experience.

Our love of all things food, especially cakes, started in Room 9 of a small town West Coast hotel with a mother who took catering for large events and weddings in her stride, with a grandmother who was a master baker and always, always had fresh cake in the house, and a green-fingered father and grandfather whose combined gardens contained bananas, figs, avocados, lemons, oranges, quinces, plums, passion fruit, grapefruit, papayas, grapes and guavas. Naturally, most of these fruits feature in our recipes.

Through being welcomed into the kitchen at an early age, baking taught us much about history (whose recipe is this?), science (the chemistry of baking), maths (measuring the ingredients – remember, measure twice, bake once!) and geography (the origin of the cake and ingredients). Our future dreams regarding travel and life centred around food. (Mari-Louis's first big assignment in Home Economics at school saw her create a Victorian Tea for Princess Caroline of Monaco. In later life she came quite close, serving royalty on a private yacht in Monte Carlo.)

For our parent's birthdays we would always cook up a storm, down to writing out menus from the fictional Cali-Mari Hotel. When we started travelling, our letters and calls to each other were first and foremost about food we had tasted in the different countries we found ourselves in.

They say if you get far enough away, you will be on your way back home. Today we find ourselves back in the Mother City after all these years, having called many countries home and fallen in love with their baked goods. Thus began Cakebread, the result of our lifelong need to do something together in the food industry. Our business has two branches: one as food stylists on commercials and for magazines, the other as designers of bespoke cakes for weddings, birthdays and corporate events. We believe that we design dreams and that our style reflects both our roots and contemporary ideas. We call it 'church bazaar meets high fashion'.

At Cakebread, our little boutique bakery, the aim is always to give our customers a product with this same distinct home-made feel. None of those replicate-a-thousand-times-a-day supermarket cakes for us. No cake looks exactly the same as the next. We believe imperfection is perfection, as long as there is love in the cake. We believe that this is why our cakes taste so delicious. We believe that taste always matters more than anything.

We believe cake baked with real butter, full-cream milk, sugar and fresh eggs in the warmth and comfort of your own kitchen is a lot healthier than shop-bought versions containing margarine, palm oils, emulsifiers, preservatives, stabilizers and modified this-and-that. Read the label on a packaged cake on your next visit to the supermarket, and you will realize why home baking is back with a vengeance.

Go get that apron on! Use your hands and lick the bowl!

So here, then, is our world in cakes . . .

Cupcake Revolution

Toffee Cupcakes with Soft Centres

Fiercely masculine on the outside, when you break this cupcake open you'll see the charmingly soft underbelly of a true gentleman. This charmer has all the yummy ingredients of an English sticky toffee pudding.

1¹/₂ cups (210 g) self-raising flour
²/₃ cup (135 g) brown sugar
¹/₂ cup (125 ml) milk
1 egg
1 tsp (5 ml) vanilla essence
45 g butter, at room temperature
1¹/₄ cups (150 g) chopped dates
8 caramel toffees

Preheat the oven to 180 °C.
Line a muffin pan with 8 paper cups.
In a medium bowl, combine the flour and sugar.
In the bowl of an electric mixer, with a paddle attachment, beat the milk, egg, vanilla essence and butter together for 2–3 minutes, until smooth and pale. Stir this batter into the flour mixture, then fold in the dates. Spoon the batter equally into the 8 cups, and push a caramel into the centre of each. Bake for 25 minutes. Remove from the oven and leave to cool for a few minutes in the pan. Turn out the cupcakes onto a wire rack and allow to cool before topping each with Meringue Buttercream with Brown Sugar and a shard of sugar, if using.

MERINGUE BUTTERCREAM WITH BROWN SUGAR

4 egg whites, room temperature
1 cup (170 g) dark brown sugar
190 g butter, softened

Over a double boiler, whisk the egg whites and sugar together for 4 minutes until the sugar has dissolved and the mixture is hot to the touch.

Pour the mixture into the mixing bowl of an electric mixer with a whisk attachment. Whisk on high for 5 minutes. Gradually add the butter (a little bit at a time), beating well after each addition. Beat on low for another 2–3 minutes. Use immediately.

SUGAR SHARDS (OPTIONAL)

a handful pumpkin seeds
1 cup (200 g) sugar
¹/₄ cup (65 ml) water

Sprinkle a Silpad or a clean baking tray with the pumpkin seeds.

Into a saucepan, set over low heat, add the sugar and water, but do not stir. Allow the mixture to caramelize (10–12 minutes). Pour the caramel in swirls over the pumpkin seeds. Leave to cool, then break into shards.

MAKES 8

White Chocolate Cupcakes with a Raspberry Smash

Sweet dreams are made of this feminine but feisty rouged number.

1¹/₂ cups (210 g) flour
1 tsp (5 ml) baking powder
¹/₂ tsp (2.5 ml) salt
100 g white chocolate, chopped
75 g butter, softened
³/₄ cup (150 g) sugar
2 eggs
1 tsp (5 ml) vanilla essence
1 cup + 1 Tbsp (265 ml) milk

Preheat the oven to 170 °C.
Prepare a couple of muffin pans with 18 paper cups.
In a medium bowl, sift together the flour,
baking powder and salt. Set aside.
In a double boiler, melt the chocolate until smooth. Set aside.
In a large bowl, cream together the butter and sugar until
light in colour. Beat in the eggs, one at a time.
Follow this with the melted white chocolate and vanilla essence.
Alternately add the flour mixture and the milk,
always ending with the flour. Mix until just combined.
Divide the batter evenly into the paper cups and bake for
20–25 minutes, or until the middles spring back when lightly
pressed. Cool on a wire rack. Ice the cupcakes
with Smashed Berry Cream Cheese.

SMASHED BERRY CREAM CHEESE

125 g fresh raspberries
1 tub (230 g) mascarpone cheese, softened
1 Tbsp (15 ml) icing sugar, sifted

In a medium bowl, crush the raspberries with a fork,
and then fold in the cheese and icing sugar. Mascarpone
discolours with time so it's best to serve the cupcakes
immediately after decorating.

MAKES 18

Vanilla Cupcakes

PURE! SPICY! **DELICATE!**

125 g butter, softened
125 g castor sugar
2 eggs
1 tsp (5 ml) vanilla essence
1 cup (140 g) self-raising flour
2 Tbsp (30 ml) milk

Preheat the oven to 180 °C. Line a muffin pan with 12 paper cups. In a mixing bowl, beat the butter and sugar until pale in colour. Add the eggs, one at a time, followed by the vanilla. Sift in half the flour, add the milk and then the remaining flour. Mix well. Spoon the batter equally into the paper cups and bake for 16–18 minutes. Leave to cool in the pan. Once cool, pipe your icing of choice onto the cupcakes.

BUTTERCREAM ICING
125 g butter, softened
1¹/₂ cups (210 g) icing sugar, sifted
2 Tbsp (30 ml) milk
1 tsp (5 ml) vanilla essence
food colouring of choice

In the bowl of an electric mixer, with a paddle attachment, beat the butter until pale in colour and creamy. Add the icing sugar and half of the milk. Mix well, then add the vanilla essence and food colouring (to the desired shade). If the mixture is too firm, add the rest of the milk and beat until it reaches your desired consistency.

MERINGUE ICING
4 egg whites, at room temperature
1 cup (200 g) sugar
a pinch salt
a drop food colouring of choice

In the heatproof bowl of an electric mixer, combine the egg whites, sugar and salt. Set the bowl over a pan of simmering water and hand-whisk continuously for 3–5 minutes until the sugar has dissolved and the mixture is hot to the touch.

Attach the bowl to the electric mixer with the whisk attachment, and beat on low for 2 minutes. Add a drop of food colouring, then beat on high for a further 5 minutes until mixture has cooled down and stiff peaks form. Use immediately.

MAKES 12

Chocolate Cupcakes

These are the fluffiest, most flavourful chocolate cupcakes you will ever bake. Each time we make them we are astounded by the light-as-air quality of these beauties. They look equally at home at kiddies' parties with playful decorations, or at adult parties and weddings, paired with strawberries, gooseberries, raspberries or even pomegranate seeds.

2 cups (400 g) sugar
1³/₄ cups (245 g) flour
³/₄ cup (90 g) cocoa powder
1¹/₂ tsp (7.5 ml) baking powder
1¹/₂ tsp (7.5 ml) bicarbonate of soda
1 tsp (5 ml) salt
2 eggs, at room temperature
1 cup (250 ml) milk
¹/₂ cup (125 ml) vegetable oil
2 tsp (10 ml) vanilla essence
1 cup (250 ml) boiling water

Preheat the oven to 180 °C.
Prepare muffin pans with 18–24 paper cups.
In the bowl of an electric mixer, mix together the sugar, flour, cocoa powder, baking powder, bicarbonate of soda and salt. Add the eggs, milk, oil and vanilla essence. Beat for 2 minutes on medium speed. Stir in the boiling water – the batter should be runny.
Pour the batter into the paper cups in equal measures. Bake for 10–12 minutes. Leave to cool completely before topping with Chocolate Buttercream Icing.

CHOCOLATE BUTTERCREAM ICING

125 g butter, softened
²/₃ cup (80 g) cocoa powder
2¹/₂ cups (350 g) icing sugar, sifted
¹/₃ cup (80 ml) milk
1 tsp (5 ml) vanilla essence

Into the bowl of an electric mixer, add the butter, then stir in the cocoa powder. Adding a little of each at a time, add the icing sugar and milk, beating on medium speed until it reaches spreading consistency. Stir in a little more milk if required. Finally, add the vanilla essence.

MAKES 18–24

Hot Chocolate Chilli Cupcakes

Oh man! Where do we start with this one? We love it for so many reasons. Because it contains no rising agent, you can keep this batter refrigerated for days, whipping it out for those surprise guests. Minutes later these same guests will think of you as a baking god/goddess when the molten chocolate centre runs as they bite into the cupcake. The look of disbelief will grow when the beautiful spicy aftertaste hits them. Voilà! Instant talk of the town. (Note: This recipe is very mild; we double up on the chilli for ours.)

185 g dark chocolate, best quality
185 g butter, cubed
1 tsp (5 ml) dried chilli flakes or 1 fresh chilli, finely chopped
  (seeds included)
3 egg yolks, lightly beaten
¹/₃ cup (50 g) flour
4 eggs
¹/₃ cup (70 g) castor sugar

Preheat the oven to 180 °C.

Grease 12 large dariole moulds or ramekins (8 cm).

In a double boiler, melt the chocolate and butter together until smooth. Remove from the heat and stir in the chilli flakes and then the egg yolks and flour.

In the bowl of an electric mixer, with the whisk attachment, beat the eggs and sugar together until light and fluffy. Fold the egg mixture into the chocolate mixture.

Bake for 10 minutes. (Do not feel tempted to leave in longer as this one sets outside the oven.) Let stand for 5 minutes. Gently run a knife around the edge of each cake and remove each one. As the cakes have a soft centre, remember to place them flat on their bottoms. Serve warm.

OPTIONAL: Decorate with melted chocolate and fresh chillies.

MAKES 12

Chai Tea Cupcakes

We love playing around with flavours and thought the combination of cinnamon, cardamom, cloves, pepper and ginger found in chai tea would make for a lovely spicy cake. We were so right.

375 g butter
1¹/₂ cups (300 g) sugar
¹/₂ cup (70 g) chai tea powder
5 eggs, at room temperature
¹/₂ tsp (2.5 ml) vanilla essence
3 cups (420 g) cake flour
1 tsp (5 ml) ground cinnamon
1 tsp (5 ml) baking powder
¹/₂ tsp (2.5 ml) bicarbonate of soda
¹/₂ tsp (2.5 ml) salt
1 cup (250 ml) buttermilk

Preheat the oven to 180 °C. Line a muffin pan with 18 paper cups. In the bowl of an electric mixer, with a paddle attachment, cream the butter, sugar and chai. Add the eggs, one at a time, scraping down the sides of the bowl regularly. Add vanilla. Sift the flour, cinnamon, baking powder, bicarb and salt, then add to the butter mixture, alternately with buttermilk, starting and ending with the flour. Divide the batter between the paper cups. Bake for 20–25 minutes. Leave to cool before decorating with Cinnamon Buttercream Icing and gold leaf (optional).

CINNAMON BUTTERCREAM ICING
125 g butter, softened
1¹/₂ cups (210 g) icing sugar, sifted
2 Tbsp (30 ml) milk
2 tsp (10 ml) ground cinnamon

Beat the butter until pale and creamy. Add the icing sugar and half of the milk. Beat until combined. Add the ground cinnamon. If the mixture is too firm, add the rest of the milk and beat to the desired consistency.

MAKES 18

Coconut Cupcakes with Fresh Coconut Shavings

Fresh coconut must surely be food from the gods, with its delicious water and nutrient-rich, tasty flesh. After stripping off the husk, you will find three indentations at the top of the coconut; one of these is soft and gives way easily. Using a sharp object, pierce another hole through one of the other indentations, then turn upside down to drain the coconut water. Be sure to keep this for use in general cooking or, better still, pull out that cocktail recipe book. Once drained, simply give the coconut a good whack with a hammer. Use a potato peeler to shave the flesh into long strips.

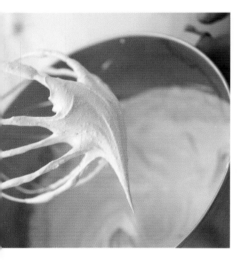

375 g butter, softened
2 cups (400 g) sugar
5 eggs
1 1/2 tsp (7.5 ml) vanilla essence
1/2 tsp (2.5 ml) almond essence
3 cups (420 g) cake flour
1 tsp (5 ml) baking powder
1/2 tsp (2.5 ml) bicarbonate of soda
1/2 tsp (2.5 ml) salt
1 cup (250 ml) buttermilk
1 cup (100 g) desiccated coconut
a handful coconut shavings

Preheat the oven to 180 °C. Line a muffin pan with 24 paper cups. In the bowl of an electric mixer, with a paddle attachment, cream the butter and sugar for approximately 5 minutes, until light and pale in colour. Add the eggs, one at a time, scraping the mixture down after each and mixing well. Add the vanilla and almond essences. In a separate bowl, sift together the flour, baking powder, bicarbonate of soda and salt. Add the dry ingredients and the buttermilk alternately to the batter, beginning and ending with the flour. Mix until well combined, then fold in the coconut. The batter should be fairly firm. Spoon the batter into the muffin cups, until three-quarters full. Bake for 20–25 minutes. Leave to cool in the pan before removing. Decorate with Meringue Icing and coconut shavings.

MERINGUE ICING
4 egg whites, room temperature
1 cup (200 g) sugar
a pinch salt

In the heatproof bowl of an electric mixer, combine the egg whites, sugar and salt. Set over a pan of simmering water, then hand-whisk continuously for 3–5 minutes until the sugar has dissolved and the mixture is hot to the touch.

Attach the bowl to the electric mixer and, with the whisk attachment, beat on low for 2 minutes, then on high for a further 5 minutes until the mixture has cooled down and stiff peaks form. Use immediately.

MAKES 24

Mojito Cupcakes

I had my first Mojito in one of Hemingway's old haunts in Havana, Cuba. The combination of rum, lime and mint have turned Mojitos into one of the world's favourite cocktails. Here is a way to combine these three ingredients with our absolute favourite – cake! – Callie

½ cup mint leaves
¾ cup (190 ml) hot milk
1½ cups (210 g) cake flour
1¼ tsp (6.25 ml) baking powder
¼ tsp (1.25 ml) bicarbonate of soda
¼ tsp (1.25 ml) salt
125 g butter
1 cup (200 g) sugar
2 eggs, at room temperature
zest of 2 limes, grated
½ tsp (2.5 ml) vanilla essence
2 Tbsp (30 ml) rum
1 quantity Meringue Icing (see page 18)

Preheat the oven to 180 °C. Line a muffin pan with 18 paper cups. Add the mint leaves to the hot milk and leave to steep for 12–15 minutes. Remove the mint; leave the milk to cool slightly.

Sift together the flour, baking powder, bicarbonate of soda and salt. In the bowl of an electric mixer, with a paddle attachment, beat the butter until creamy. Add the sugar and continue beating on medium speed for approximately 5 minutes, until the mixture becomes light and fluffy. Add the eggs, one at a time, then mix in the lime zest, vanilla essence and rum. On a low speed, add the flour mixture and milk alternately, ending with the flour. Spoon the mixture into the muffin cups until half-full. Bake for 20 minutes. Allow to cool before piping on meringue icing. Decorate with slices of lime and mint leaves.

MAKES 18

Classic Cakes

Mrs M's Angel Food Cake

The lightest, whitest, airiest of all cakes, it is easy to see why it is likened to angel's food. Our recipe dates from the time Mari-Louis was a private chef aboard a yacht (cruising the Hamptons) owned by a Mr and Mrs M. For confidentiality reasons we always called the yacht owners by their initials. This is a cake for high days and holidays, and always evokes memories of blue waters and long summer nights. It requires a little effort, but the result is worth it.

1 cup (140 g) flour
12 egg whites, at room temperature
1 Tbsp (15 ml) warm water
1/2 tsp (2.5 ml) salt
1 tsp (5 ml) cream of tartar
1 1/2 cups (300 g) castor sugar
1 tsp (5 ml) vanilla essence
icing sugar for dusting
berries (your choice) for serving

Preheat the oven to 180 °C. Use a 25 cm angel food cake pan. Very important: do not coat the pan.

In a small mixing bowl, sift the flour four times. Set aside.

In the bowl of an electric mixer, with the whisk attachment, beat the egg whites and the warm water on low speed until foamy. Add the salt and the cream of tartar. Increase the speed and beat until soft peak stage. Add the sugar, one tablespoon at a time. Beat until the mixture is stiff and glossy. Beat in the vanilla essence. Sift the flour into the mixture and fold in gently.

Spoon the batter into the angel food cake pan. The mixture will fill most of the pan. Bake for 35–40 minutes, or until the cake springs back when lightly pressed. Invert the pan over the neck of a bottle and leave to cool completely (about 1 hour). Gently loosen the sides with a sharp knife and invert the cake onto a wire rack. Dust with icing sugar and serve with berries of choice.

Devil's Food Cake

DARK! MOODY! **SINFUL!**

Chocolate cake with swirly dollops of chocolate ganache. It was probably named thus because when it first appeared, Angel's Food Cake with its soft, white hues was already famous.

1¼ cups (175 g) flour
½ cup (60 g) unsweetened cocoa powder
1 tsp (5 ml) bicarbonate of soda
¼ tsp (1.25 ml) baking powder
½ tsp (2.5 ml) salt
60 g butter
1½ cups (300 g) sugar
3 eggs, at room temperature
1 tsp (5 ml) vanilla essence
½ cup (125 ml) buttermilk, at room temperature
½ cup (125 ml) strong coffee

CHOCOLATE GANACHE
1½ cups (375 ml) cream
350 g dark chocolate, finely chopped

In a saucepan over medium heat, heat the cream. Remove from the heat, then add the chocolate. Let it melt slightly before stirring to a smooth gloss. Set aside to cool.

Preheat the oven to 180 °C. Lightly grease 2 x 23-cm cake pans and line the base with baking paper.
In a medium bowl, sift together the flour, cocoa powder, bicarbonate of soda, baking powder and salt.
In the bowl of an electric mixer, with a paddle attachment, cream the butter and sugar on high speed until pale in colour. Add the eggs, one at a time. Add the vanilla essence and mix well.
In a separate bowl, combine the buttermilk and coffee. With the mixer on low speed, gradually add the flour mixture and the buttermilk mixture alternately to the creamed butter and sugar, ending with the flour mixture. Divide the batter between the two pans. Smooth the tops and bake for 30 minutes, or until the centre springs back when lightly pressed.
Leave to cool on a rack for 10 minutes, then remove from the pans and set aside to cool completely.
Place one cake on a serving plate, flat-side up. Ice the top of that layer with ganache. Place the remaining layer on top, flat-side up, then ice the top and sides with the remaining ganache.

Black Forest Roulade

This is definitely one of our guilty pleasures. Most recipes for a Black Forest cake differ in their ingredients, possibly as a result of an abundance of cheap supermarket versions. The secret to a successful Black Forest cake is to use the best ingredients available, i.e. quality cherries, good cocoa and excellent Kirsch. A beautiful, over-the-top confectionery, Black Forest Roulade will always attract attention.

1 cup (250 ml) cherry juice
½ cup (100 g) sugar
4 Tbsp (60 ml) Kirsch liqueur
2 cups (500 ml) fresh cream
½ cup (100 g) castor sugar
2 Tbsp (30 ml) castor sugar
6 large eggs, separated
2 Tbsp (30 ml) cocoa powder
¼ cup (35 g) flour
¾ cup (150 g) sugar
1 cup (100 g) maraschino cherries or fresh, pitted cherries
extra cocoa powder to serve
fresh cherries to decorate

In a medium saucepan combine the cherry juice and sugar. Stir over a low heat until the sugar has dissolved. Boil for 45 minutes, until it forms a syrup. Add half the Kirsch liqueur. Set aside.

Using an electric mixer, with a whisk attachment, beat the cream and ½ cup of castor sugar until stiff. Stir in the remaining Kirsch liqueur. Set aside.

Preheat the oven to 170 °C. Line a swiss roll pan with baking paper, ensuring that you grease the sides. Dust a clean dishcloth with the 2 Tbsp of castor sugar.

In the bowl of an electric mixer, with the whisk attachment, beat the egg yolks until thick and very pale. Sift the cocoa powder and the flour into the egg yolks. Fold in until just combined.

In a clean bowl, and using the whisk attachment, beat the egg whites until foamy. Increase the speed and gradually add the sugar. Beat on high speed until stiff peaks form. Gently fold this into the batter.

Spoon the batter into the prepared swiss roll pan, ensuring that it spreads into the corners. Bake for 15 minutes, until the centre of the cake springs back when gently touched. Immediately turn the cake out onto the dusted dishcloth. Carefully peel off the baking paper and roll the cake up lengthwise, using the cloth as a tool to help. Transfer the log to a wire rack and be sure to set it down on its seam until completely cool.

Carefully unroll the log and sprinkle with the cherry syrup. Spoon the cream filling over, and add the cherries (reserve some as decoration). Roll up again and refrigerate until ready to serve.

To serve, dust with cocoa powder and decorate with fresh cherries.

Carrot Cake

Healthy, moist and spicy! Full of nuts and loaded with beta-carotene, this cake is our friend Moira's family recipe. It's versatile and forgiving, and even freezes beautifully – a real crowd pleaser.

2¹/₂ cups (350 g) flour

1¹/₂ tsp (7.5 ml) bicarbonate of soda

2 tsp (10 ml) baking powder

1 Tbsp (15 ml) ground cinnamon

1 Tbsp (15 ml) mixed spice

2 cups (400 g) sugar

1¹/₄ cups (315 ml) vegetable oil

¹/₄ cup (65 ml) apricot jam, melted

4 eggs

2 cups grated carrot

1 cup crushed pineapple, drained and juice reserved

¹/₂ cup (60 g) nuts of choice , chopped

2 x quantity Meringue Icing (see page 18)

Preheat the oven to 180 °C. Grease and line 3 x 18 cm cake pans or prepare muffin pans with 24 paper cups.
In a mixing bowl, sift the flour, bicarbonate of soda, baking powder, cinnamon and mixed spice together.
Add the sugar, oil, jam and eggs. Mix well.
Stir in the carrot, pineapple and nuts.
Bake the cakes for 30–35 minutes, or the cupcakes for 15–20 minutes. Leave to cool on a wire rack, and then remove from the pan.
To assemble, spread the first two cake layers with the Cream Cheese Icing and stack. Ice the cake all around with generous amounts of the Meringue Icing.

CREAM CHEESE ICING

1 tub (250 g) firm cream cheese

250 g butter, softened

2 cups (280 g) icing sugar, sifted

1 tsp (5 ml) vanilla essence

In the bowl of an electric mixer with the paddle attachment, beat the cream cheese and butter until light and fluffy. Add the icing sugar and beat through. Add the vanilla essence and beat until just combined. We find it is best to let this icing rest in the refrigerator for about 20 minutes before using.

HINT: Substitute the carrot with sweet potato or apple for splendid variations.

MAKES 1 LARGE CAKE OR 24 CUPCAKES

Lime and Almond Cake

Traditionally this is baked as an orange or mandarin cake. In this interpretation of 'going green', we decided to use limes for our version. We fell in love with limes while sailing the Caribbean, where every island seems to have a slightly different variety. Our favourites are the really small and tart ones.

3 limes
1 cup (200 g) castor sugar
6 eggs, at room temperature
2 cups (230 g) ground almonds
1/4 cup (50 g) sugar
1/4 cup (65 ml) water
zest of 2 limes
mascarpone cheese to serve

Preheat the oven to 160 °C. Grease a 23-cm spring form cake pan. Cover the limes with water in a medium saucepan and bring to the boil. Simmer for 2 hours, adding water when necessary to keep the fruit covered at all times. Drain the limes and leave to cool. Cut the limes open and remove any pips. Purée the limes, including the peel, in a food processor.

In a large bowl, whisk the castor sugar and eggs together until well mixed. Add the ground almonds and lime pulp. Stir thoroughly. Pour the mixture into the prepared pan and bake for 1 hour, or until the centre of the cake is firm to the touch and comes away from the edges of the pan. Remove from the oven and leave to cool in the pan.

In a saucepan over low heat, dissolve the sugar in the water. Add the lime zest, then boil the mixture until it just starts to caramelize. Remove the zest with a fork and leave it to cool on a plate. Serve with mascarpone cheese and the caramelized citrus zest.

OPTIONAL: Dust with icing sugar and then, using a heated metal skewer, score the top of the cake with patterns of your choice.

Hummingbird Cake

In all our searches and trials this recipe is virtually the same, a true reflection of a classic. The reason for the name is a mystery but the cake is very well known throughout the American South. We think it is so called because the HHMMM sound guests make when first tasting this cake sounds just like a hummingbird.

3 cups (420 g) flour
2 cups (400 g) sugar
1 tsp (5 ml) bicarbonate of soda
1 tsp (5 ml) ground cinnamon
1 tsp (5 ml) salt
4 eggs, beaten
1½ cups (375 ml) vegetable oil
1 can (400 g) crushed pineapple, not drained
1 cup (120 g) chopped nuts of choice
2 cups (about 6) mashed bananas
1½ tsp (7.5 ml) vanilla essence
1 x quantity Cream Cheese Icing (see page 31)

Preheat the oven to 180 °C. Grease and line 3 x 23-cm cake pans. In a large bowl, sift the flour, sugar, bicarbonate of soda, cinnamon and salt together. Add the eggs and oil and stir until well combined. Stir in the pineapple and juice, the nuts, bananas and vanilla.

Spoon the batter into the cake pans, and then bake for 25–30 minutes. Let the cakes cool in the pans for 10 minutes, and then turn them out onto racks to cool completely. Ice each layer of cake and stack them before icing all around with large gentle swirls.

VARIATION: For an exotic option, replace the pineapple with a can of liquidized mangoes.

Victoria Sponge Cake

My first ever large cake, as taught to me by Mrs Goldie, my Home Economics teacher back in 1982. For my practical exam I did a 'Victorian Tea', with Princess Caroline of Monaco as guest (well, that was what was written on the name card for the seating arrangements). While Princess Caroline could not make it that day, I was lucky enough to serve a member of the British Royal Family on a yacht in Monte Carlo many years later. – Mari-Louis

225 g butter
1¼ cups (250 g) castor sugar
4 eggs
1½ cups (210 g) flour
1 tsp (5 ml) baking powder
2 Tbsp (30 ml) milk
1 tsp (5 ml) vanilla essence

⁴/₅ cup (200 ml) cream
1 Tbsp (15 ml) castor sugar
1 tsp (5 ml) vanilla essence

3 Tbsp (45 ml) raspberry or apricot jam
icing sugar for dusting

Preheat the oven to 180 °C. Line and grease 2 x 20 cm or 3 x 15 cm cake pans.

In the bowl of an electric mixer, with the paddle attachment, cream the butter and castor sugar until light and fluffy. Add the eggs, one at a time, remembering to scrape down the sides regularly. Sift the flour and baking powder together. Fold in the flour mixture, milk and vanilla essence until the mixture is smooth.

Pour equal amounts of cake batter into the prepared pans and bake for 25–30 minutes, or until golden and the centre of the cake springs back when gently pressed. Invert onto a wire rack and cool completely.

In a clean bowl whisk the cream, castor sugar and vanilla essence until stiff peaks form.

To assemble, sandwich the layers together with jam and cream. Dust the top with icing sugar and serve.

Mello Yello

Since childhood, we have referred to yellow cake as Mello Yello, perhaps because of the old Donovan song, maybe because it rhymes, or simply because it could be that it is so forgivingly easy to make and pair with various flavours and toppings. Ultimately, the reason for its name isn't important, but we do remember loving it every time. This cake is like a blank canvas and ultra easy to make, so feel free to experiment with more difficult toppings with the time you save baking.

2^1/$_4$ cups (315 g) flour, sifted
1^1/$_3$ cups (270 g) sugar
1 Tbsp (15 ml) baking powder
^{1}/$_2$ tsp (2.5 ml) salt
115 g butter
1 cup (250 ml) milk
1 tsp (5 ml) vanilla essence
2 eggs

Preheat the oven to 180 °C. Grease and line a 20 cm cake pan or prepare a muffin pan with 10 paper cups.
Now here comes the joy. Into the bowl of an electric mixer, with the paddle attachment, simply add all of the ingredients and mix until just combined. Spoon the batter into the prepared pans or paper cups and bake for 30–35 minutes for a large cake, or 15–20 minutes for cupcakes.
Cool completely before topping with the Caramel Icing and decorate with the Hokey Pokey.

CARAMEL ICING

125 g butter, diced
1 cup (170 g) brown sugar
^{1}/$_3$ cup (80 ml) milk
1^1/$_2$ cups (210 g) icing sugar, sifted

In a small saucepan, combine the butter, brown sugar and milk. Stir until the sugar has dissolved, and then bring to a simmer for 3 minutes. Remove from heat and stir in the icing sugar. Use immediately.

HOKEY POKEY

4 Tbsp (60 ml) sugar
4 Tbsp (60 ml) golden syrup
1 tsp (5 ml) bicarbonate of soda
^{1}/$_4$ cup (30 g) hazelnuts

In a medium saucepan, bring the sugar and syrup slowly to boiling point, stirring gently all the time. Once it starts to boil, stir every few minutes for about 7 minutes. Remove from the heat and add the bicarbonate of soda. Stir in quickly (be careful as it froths quite a bit). Pour the mixture onto a greased baking tray and press the nuts into it. Setting time is less than a minute. Cool completely, and then break into shards. Store in an airtight container.

MAKES 1 CAKE OR 10 CUPCAKES

Chocolate Mousse Cake

This cake takes us back to our days in Turkey; it's from the restaurant Turkay in beautiful Marmaris.

CHOCOLATE CAKE

2 cups (400 g) sugar
1³/₄ cups (245 g) flour
³/₄ cup (90 g) cocoa powder
1¹/₂ tsp (7.5 ml) baking powder
1¹/₂ tsp (7.5 ml) bicarbonate of soda
1 tsp (5 ml) salt
2 eggs, at room temperature
1 cup (250 ml) milk
¹/₂ cup (125 ml) vegetable oil
2 tsp (10 ml) vanilla essence
1 cup (250 ml) boiling water

Preheat the oven to 180 °C. Grease and line a 26-cm cake pan. In the bowl of an electric mixer, fitted with a paddle attachment, mix together the sugar, flour, cocoa powder, baking powder, bicarbonate of soda and salt. Add the eggs, milk, oil and vanilla essence. Beat for 2 minutes on medium speed. Stir in the boiling water – the batter should be runny. Pour the batter into the prepared cake pan and bake for 30–35 minutes, or until the centre of the cake springs back when lightly pressed. Cool in the pan for 10 minutes before turning out.

CHOCOLATE BANDS: Measure the circumference and height of the finished cake and add a few centimetres to both (to create an overlap). Cut baking paper to these dimensions and flatten out on a clean work surface. Melt chocolate (we prefer dark) in a double boiler. Pour the chocolate onto the baking paper. Use a spatula to smooth out the chocolate and remember to go over all the edges as shown above. After a minute you will notice the chocolate loses some of its gloss. It is now ready to wrap around the cake, chocolate side against the cake. Refrigerate the cake immediately and only remove the baking paper just before serving.

CHOCOLATE MOUSSE

330 g dark chocolate, grated
150 g butter, cut into pieces
³/₅ cup (150 ml) milk
2¹/₂ cups (625 ml) cream

In a mixing bowl, combine the chocolate and butter.

In a saucepan, bring the milk to boiling point, then pour it over the chocolate and butter mixture. Stir until dissolved. Leave the mixture to cool to room temperature.

Whip the cream until soft peaks form, and then fold it into the chocolate mixture.

CHOCOLATE GANACHE

300 g dark chocolate
1 cup (250 ml) cream

In a double boiler, melt the chocolate and cream together, stirring until smooth. Leave to cool to room temperature – it should thicken slightly, but still have a pouring consistency.

TO ASSEMBLE

Grease a 26-cm spring form cake pan. Cut the chocolate cake into 3-cm high layers and ease one layer into the spring form pan. Cover with chocolate mousse and refrigerate for 10 minutes before repeating the process for each layer. Refrigerate overnight.

Make the ganache. Remove the cake from the pan and pour the ganache over the cake, also covering the sides. Refrigerate again until the ganache has set.

For added effect, follow the method for Chocolate Bands described alongside.

Bake and Serve

Pomegranate Glaze Cake

Once more back to the garden of our childhood home. Pomegranates remain the most surprising of fruits, nothing special when you see them hanging on the tree, but break them open and be dazzled by hundreds of juicy, jewel-like seeds.

250 g butter, softened
2 cups (400 g) castor sugar
2 cups (280 g) self-raising flour, sifted
1 tsp (5 ml) baking powder
4 eggs
1 tsp (5 ml) vanilla essence
seeds of 2 pomegranates to decorate

Preheat the oven to 180 °C. Grease and line an 18-cm round cake pan or a medium Bundt pan.

In the bowl of an electric mixer, with a paddle attachment, cream the butter and castor sugar until light and creamy. Add the flour, baking powder, eggs and vanilla essence, and beat until the batter is smooth and pale.

Spoon the mixture into the pan and bake for 45 minutes or until the centre of the cake springs back when lightly pressed. (For this recipe we chose an unusual shape for our cake and to that end we overfill our pan. You are welcome to divide your batter between two pans for a more traditional layer cake, just remember to reduce baking time to 35 minutes.)

Remove the cake from the oven and let it rest for 10 minutes. Remove the cake from the pan and place on a serving plate. Spike all over with a thin skewer, and then drizzle the cake with the pomegranate glaze. Decorate with the pomegranate seeds and serve while still warm.

POMEGRANATE GLAZE

1 cup (250 ml) pomegranate juice or 200 ml ($4/5$ cup) water with 50 ml grenadine
$1/2$ cup (100 g) sugar
a drop red food colouring (if needed)
1 cup pomegranate seeds

Heat the pomegranate juice and sugar in a medium saucepan over medium heat. Stir until the sugar has dissolved, and then bring to the boil. Reduce the heat and simmer for 10–12 minutes, or until syrupy. Remove from the heat and add the food colouring and seeds.

SECRET: Brush the sides of the cake with the glaze for a more dramatic effect.

Individual Blueberry Coconut Cakes

Blueberries just weren't part of our food chain when we grew up. As a matter of fact, nothing blue was. It was only as we started travelling that we had the pleasure of tasting this amazing little indigo super fruit. With globalization this gem of a berry has made its way to all corners and we can't stop to find excuses not to try it in our favourite recipes.

110 g butter, softened
³/₄ cup (150 g) sugar
2 eggs
5 Tbsp (75 ml) cream
1 tsp (5 ml) vanilla essence
1 cup (140 g) self-raising flour
¹/₄ tsp (1.25 ml) salt
1 cup (100 g) desiccated coconut
¹/₂ cup (50 g) blueberries
¹/₂ cup (60 g) mixed nuts

Preheat the oven to 180 °C. Grease 6–8 large dariole moulds or 8-cm diameter ramekins.

In the bowl of an electric mixer, with a paddle attachment, beat together the butter and sugar until creamy. Add the eggs, one at a time, then add the cream and vanilla essence, remembering to scrape down the sides of the bowl regularly.

In a separate bowl, sift the flour and salt together. Add this to the butter mixture and beat on low speed until just combined. Stir in ¹/₂ cup coconut, the blueberries and the mixed nuts.

Divide the batter equally into the moulds or ramekins and smooth the tops. Sprinkle with the remaining coconut. Bake for 20–25 minutes. Serve while still warm.

MAKES 6–8 CAKES

New York Cheesecake

We are both huge fans of the Cheesecake Factory, that splendid restaurant, bakery and bar chain in the USA, whose menu features something in excess of 54 versions of cheesecake. It is, however, the New York recipe that gets our nod. All regular visitors to New York usually have some fashionable clothing outlet as their first stop. True to form, we always go in search of something sweet.

CRUST
85 g butter
280 g digestive biscuits, crushed

FILLING
900 g cream cheese, best quality
250 g sugar
3 Tbsp (45 ml) flour
3 eggs + 1 egg yolk
1 cup (250 ml) sour cream
1½ tsp (7.5 ml) vanilla essence

TOPPING
1 cup (250 ml) sour cream
1 Tbsp (15 ml) castor sugar
juice from 1 lemon

Preheat the oven to 180 °C. Grease and line a 23-cm spring form cake pan.

For the crust, melt the butter in the microwave or a saucepan, and then stir it into the crushed biscuits in a large bowl. Neatly press the mixture onto the base and sides of the cake pan and bake for 10 minutes. Cool while preparing the filling. Increase the oven setting to 230 °C.

In the bowl of an electric mixer, with the paddle attachment, beat the cream cheese until fluffy. Add the sugar and flour and continue beating for another 3 minutes. Add the eggs and yolk, one at a time, remembering to scrape down the sides of the bowl regularly. Stir in the sour cream and vanilla essence.

Pour the filling into the prepared pan, and then bake for 10 minutes. Reduce the oven setting to 110 °C and bake for a further 30 minutes. Switch off the oven and open the door. Leave the cake to cool in the oven, at least 2 hours.

In a medium bowl, stir the sour cream, castor sugar and lemon juice together until the sugar has dissolved. Pour over the cooled cheesecake and refrigerate overnight before gently loosening the sides and removing the cake.

BAKER'S SECRET: To make sure all the crumbs are fine, push them through a sieve.

Apricot Upside~down Cake

Upside-down cakes always looks so lovingly home-made – real cake-and-a-glass-of-milk stuff. Use any fruit in season, although we prefer something tart, such as apricots, rhubarb or plums.

75 g butter
³/₄ cup (150 g) dark brown sugar
10 fresh apricots, halved and pitted
¹/₂ tsp (2.5 ml) ground cinnamon
¹/₄ tsp (1.25 ml) ground nutmeg
125 g butter, softened
1¹/₄ cups (250 g) castor sugar
2 eggs
1 tsp (5 ml) vanilla essence
1 cup (140 g) self-raising flour
2 Tbsp (30 ml) milk

APRICOT GLAZE (OPTIONAL)
10 apricots, halved and pitted
¹/₄ cup (40 g) brown sugar
2 Tbsp (30 ml) water

In a saucepan over medium heat, combine the apricots, brown sugar and water. Stir until the sugar has dissolved and apricots are glazed. Pour over the turned out cake.

Preheat the oven to 180 °C. Grease and line a 23-cm cake pan. In a small saucepan, combine the 75 g butter and the brown sugar. Stir until the sugar has dissolved and the mixture starts to bubble. Add the fruit and spices, and stir for 5 minutes over medium heat. Pour the mixture into the cake pan. Remember that the bottom will become the top once the cake is turned out, so take time to arrange the fruit accordingly.

In a mixing bowl, beat the 125 g butter and castor sugar together until pale in colour. Add the eggs, one at a time, and then stir in the vanilla essence. Sift in half the flour, add the milk, and then the remaining flour.

Spoon the batter over the fruit mixture in the cake pan and bake for 1 hour and 15 minutes, or until the centre springs back when lightly pressed. Leave to cool in the pan.

Turn out and serve with a dollop of mascarpone cheese.

Estee's Sticky Date Loaf

One of our mother's favourite treats. She still eats hers with a generous spread of farm butter.

2 cups (300 g) pitted dates, chopped
1 tsp (5 ml) bicarbonate of soda
1 cup (250 ml) boiling water
2 eggs
1 cup (200 g) sugar
20 g butter
1 tsp (5 ml) vanilla essence
1³/₄ cups (245 g) flour
1 tsp (5 ml) salt
2 tsp (10 ml) baking powder
1³/₄ cups (210 g) walnuts, chopped
whole dates to decorate

Preheat the oven to 180 °C. Grease and line two medium loaf pans.

In a medium bowl, combine the chopped dates and bicarbonate of soda with the boiling water.

In the bowl of an electric mixer, with a paddle attachment, beat the eggs and sugar together, and then add the butter and vanilla essence. Stir in the date mixture.

Sift the flour, salt and baking powder into the mixture and add 1 cup (120 g) of the nuts.

Spoon the batter into the prepared pans. Bake for 45 minutes. Halfway through baking, press the rest of the nuts and the whole dates lightly into the top of the loaves.

MAKES 2 LOAVES

Sour Cream Streussel Cake

A perfect tea-time cake for those with a fear of icing. We pack ours full of fruit and nuts to ensure it stays moist and delicious for up to a week.

1¼ cups (150 g) coarsely chopped macadamia nuts

1¼ cups (250 g) brown sugar

4 tsp (20 ml) ground cinnamon

4 tsp (20 ml) cocoa powder

½ cup (100 g) dried cranberries

3 cups (420 g) flour

1½ tsp (7.5 ml) bicarbonate of soda

1½ tsp (7.5 ml) baking powder

¾ tsp (3.75 ml) salt

170 g butter, at room temperature

1½ cups (300 g) white sugar

3 eggs

1 Tbsp (15 ml) vanilla essence

1½ cups (375 ml) sour cream or buttermilk

Preheat the oven to 180 °C. Grease a large Bundt pan or prepare a muffin pan with 12 paper cups. (We made 24 mini cakes – use mini cupcake pans for these.)

Mix the nuts, brown sugar, cinnamon, cocoa powder and dried cranberries together. Set aside.

In a medium bowl, sift the flour, bicarbonate of soda, baking powder and salt together. Set aside.

In the bowl of an electric mixer, beat the butter and white sugar until creamy. Beat in the eggs, one at a time. Mix in the vanilla essence. Add the flour mixture and sour cream alternately to the butter mixture, ending with the flour. Beat on high for 1 minute. Pour half of the batter into the prepared pan. Sprinkle with half of the nut mixture. Spoon the rest of the batter over. Sprinkle with the remaining nut mixture. Bake for 50–60 minutes for a large cake, 15–20 minutes for cupcakes and 10–15 minutes for mini cakes. Rest for 10 minutes before turning out.

MAKES 1 LARGE CAKE, 12 CUPCAKES OR 24 MINI CAKES

Scandinavian Apple Cake

I love the overwhelming simplicity of Scandinavian cooking. A Danish friend, Vivi, introduced me to the feast that is their Christmas and, although this is not necessarily on the menu for Christmas Eve, it certainly features prominently for the rest of their festive season. – Mari-Louis

3 Tbsp (45 ml) white cookie crumbs (pick your favourite)	pinch of salt
	1 tsp (5 ml) ground cinnamon
6 apples, peeled and cored	225 g butter, softened
juice of 1 lemon	1 cup (200 g) sugar
2 cups (280 g) flour	3 eggs
1 tsp (5 ml) baking powder	3 Tbsp (45 ml) sugar for sprinkling

Preheat the oven to 180 °C. Grease and line a round 23-cm spring form cake pan.

Sprinkle the pan with the cookie crumbs. Set aside. Cut 3 apples into small cubes, sprinkle with lemon juice and set aside. Cut the rest of the apples into slices, sprinkle with lemon juice and set aside.

In a medium bowl, sift the flour, baking powder, salt and cinnamon together.

In the bowl of an electric mixer, with a paddle attachment, cream the butter and sugar until light and fluffy. Add the eggs, one at a time, remembering to scrape down the sides of the bowl regularly. Stir in the flour mixture. Stir in the apple cubes.

Spoon the batter into the pan, and then arrange the apple slices on top of the cake. Sprinkle with the 3 Tbsp of sugar. Bake for 45 minutes, or until the centre of the cake springs back when lightly pressed.

For special occasions, serve with a cranberry sauce.

SECRET: Cutting the apple into small cubes makes for much better distribution within the cake.

Espresso Streussel Cake

We love cobblers, we love Brown Betty pudding and we love Streussel cake. So we decided to create our own cake by combining all of these. We bring our 'little Frankenstein' to life by waking it up with a shot of espresso coffee.

500 g dessert apples, peeled, cored and diced
3 Tbsp (45 ml) espresso coffee
1½ cups (210 g) flour
50 g cocoa powder
1 Tbsp (15 ml) baking powder
pinch of salt
125 g butter, softened
1 cup (200 g) sugar
1 tsp (5 ml) vanilla essence
2 eggs
2 Tbsp (30 ml) milk

STREUSSEL TOPPING
⅓ cup (50 g) flour
1 Tbsp (15 ml) cocoa powder
30 g butter, chilled
¼ cup (40 g) brown sugar
1 cup (120 g) roasted peanuts

Preheat the oven to 170 °C. Grease and line a 20-cm spring form cake pan.

In a medium bowl, combine the apples and espresso, set aside.

In another medium bowl, sift the flour, cocoa powder, baking powder and salt.

In the bowl of an electric mixer with the paddle attachment, cream the butter and sugar with the vanilla essence.

Beat in the eggs. Fold in the flour mixture, and then the milk and the apples.

Make the topping by sifting the flour and cocoa powder together. Rub the butter, flour and sugar together to form fine crumbs. Stir in the peanuts.

Spoon the cake mixture into the pan, and then sprinkle on the topping. Bake for 30 minutes, cover with foil and bake for another 15 minutes, or until a skewer inserted into the centre of the cake comes out clean. Remove from the oven and cool in the pan. Turn out and serve with whipped cream flavoured with coffee powder.

Back to Natural

Quinoa Almond Cake (Gluten Free)

Quinoa (pronounced keen-wah) is a high-protein grain with a grassy, nutty flavour that we use in salads. Here we use it as an alternative to flour to make a delicious wheat-free cake.

150 g quinoa
1½ cups (150 g) ground almonds
4 eggs, separated
1 cup (170 g) brown sugar
1 tsp (5 ml) baking powder
2 tsp (10 ml) cornflour, sifted
25 g butter, melted

Preheat the oven to 180 °C. Grease a 20-cm spring form cake pan and line the bottom with baking paper.
In separate pans, over low heat, roast the quinoa and almonds for 15–20 minutes until golden brown. In a saucepan, bring the roasted quinoa to the boil in 400 ml water, cover and simmer for 15 minutes until the grains burst. Let it cool.
In the bowl of an electric mixer, with the whisk attachment, beat the egg yolks and half of the brown sugar until pale and creamy.
In a separate bowl, beat the egg whites, the remaining brown sugar and the baking powder together until thick.
Into the egg yolk mixture, fold the quinoa, almonds and cornflour. Fold in the egg white mixture and the melted butter.
Spoon the batter into the baking pan and bake for 45 minutes, or until the centre of the cake springs back when lightly pressed. Remove from the pan and leave to cool.
Drizzle with rose petal preserve. This cake stays moist and fresh – stored at room temperature – for days.

ROSE PETAL PRESERVE
2 cups rose petals, washed and loosely packed
2 Tbsp (30 ml) lemon juice
2 cups (400 g) sugar
1½ cups (375 ml) water

Wash the petals and tear off the white parts at the base. Combine the petals and lemon juice in a saucepan. Stir over low heat with a wooden spoon until the petals start to disintegrate. Place the saucepan into a bowl of ice water to stop the cooking process and set the colour. When cooled, drain the liquid from the petals.
In a saucepan, combine the sugar and water, stirring until the sugar dissolves. Bring the syrup to a boil over high heat and add the drained petals. Simmer over low heat for 10–12 minutes, stirring until the syrup thickens. Remove the mixture from the heat and let it cool completely.

MAKES ABOUT 2 CUPS (500 ML)

Brazilian Bolo (Dairy Free)

Twice my husband took part in the Cape to Rio yacht race, which meant that twice I had the pleasure of waiting for him at the finish line. I begged a Brazilian chef for the recipe of this creamy cake and was astounded when I realized that it is completely dairy free. – Mari-Louis

2 cups (280 g) flour
¹/₂ cup (60 g) cornflour
2 tsp (10 ml) baking powder
5 eggs, separated
1³/₄ cups (350 g) sugar
1 cup (250 ml) coconut milk

Preheat the oven to 180 °C.

Grease a Bundt pan or a 23-cm round cake pan.

In a medium bowl, sift the flour, cornflour and baking powder together. Set aside.

In the bowl of an electric mixer, with the whisk attachment, beat the eggs whites until stiff peaks form. Set aside.

In a medium bowl, stir the egg yolks and sugar until just combined. Gradually add this egg yolk mixture to the egg whites, beating at medium speed until combined. On low speed, alternately add the flour mixture and the coconut milk, starting and ending with the flour mixture. Pour the batter into the prepared pan. Bake for 40 minutes, or until the centre of the cake springs back when lightly pressed. Cool in the pan for 10 minutes before inverting the cake onto a wire rack. Let cool completely, and then pour the Coconut Icing over the cake.

COCONUT ICING
2 cups (280 g) icing sugar
¹/₃ cup (80 ml) coconut milk

Gradually add icing sugar to the coconut milk, stirring continuously, until the desired consistency is achieved.

Eggless Apple and Cinnamon Cake

We first made this cake for a vegan wedding by replacing the buttermilk for an equal amount of coconut milk. The guests enjoyed it so much that the happy couple have been ordering it for every birthday since. Fresh fruit is a great addition to eggless cakes as it makes for a soft, moist cake. This recipe is also easy to halve for smaller events.

5 cups (700 g) self-raising flour
1 Tbsp (15 ml) baking powder
1 cup (200 g) sugar
2 tsp (10 ml) ground cinnamon
1 tsp (5 ml) salt
250 g butter, melted
4 Tbsp (60 ml) buttermilk
1 cup (200 g) dried cranberries
1 cup (120 g) pecan nuts
1 x large tin (765 g) pie apples
cream
3 large red apples, grated
juice of 1 lemon

Preheat the oven to 180 °C. Grease 2 x 23-cm cake pans.
In a mixing bowl sift together the flour, baking powder, sugar, cinnamon and salt. Stir in the melted butter, buttermilk, cranberries, nuts and tinned apples.
Spoon the mixture into the prepared baking pans and bake for 1–1½ hours, or until the centre of the cake is firm to the touch.
Allow to cool in the pans for 10 minutes before turning out onto a wire rack.
When cooled completely, sandwich the two layers together with the cream and top with grated apple. (Remember to squeeze the lemon juice over the apple just after grating to keep it from going brown.)

Vegan Chocolate Cake

Requests for vegan cakes are definitely on the rise. We used to get asked to come up with something different to accommodate a few guests at a wedding, but now we get vegan couples who ask for a complete feast in their preferred style of diet. These moist, rich chocolate pieces break all preconceptions and simply please everyone.

3 cups (420 g) flour
2 cups (400 g) sugar
6 Tbsp (90 ml) cocoa powder
2 tsp (10 ml) bicarbonate of soda
1 tsp (5 ml) salt
2 cups (500 ml) water
3/4 cup (190 ml) vegetable oil
2 Tbsp (30 ml) blackberry or blueberry balsamic vinegar
2 tsp (10 ml) vanilla essence

Preheat the oven to 180 °C.
Grease 6–8 dariole moulds or a 23-cm cake pan.
Sift together the flour, sugar, cocoa powder, bicarbonate of soda and salt. In a medium mixing bowl, combine the water, oil, vinegar and vanilla essence. In the mixing bowl of an electric mixer, with a paddle attachment, combine the wet and dry ingredients. Pour the batter into the dariole moulds and bake for 15–20 minutes for individual cakes, or 35–40 minutes for a large cake, or until the centres of the cakes spring back when lightly pressed. (The cakes will still be quite moist.) Decorate with Blackberries in Syrup and vegetable whip (optional).

MAKES 1 LARGE CAKE OR 6–8 INDIVIDUAL CAKES

BLACKBERRIES IN SYRUP
1/4 cup (50 g) sugar
2 Tbsp (30 ml) water
1 cup fresh blackberries

In a small saucepan, dissolve the sugar in the water. Bring to a boil until it reaches a syrupy consistency. Add the blackberries and cook until the berries start to disintegrate slightly.

Pear, Honey and Polenta Cake

This glorious yellow cake is not very sweet and we therefore often serve it with crème fraîche and fabulous orange blossom honey. For more extravagant affairs you can top it with caramelized pears.

125 g carrots, grated
1½ cups (200 g) dried pears, chopped
⁴/₅ cup (200 ml) pear juice
125 g butter, softened
¾ cup (90 g) gluten-free flour (we use quinoa flour)
2½ tsp (12.5 ml) baking powder
1 cup (150 g) instant polenta
3 eggs, lightly beaten
zest of 1 lemon
zest of 1 lime
2 Tbsp (30 ml) honey
1 tsp (5 ml) vanilla essence
2 firm pears, to decorate
lemon juice for sprinkling

Preheat the oven to 180 °C.

Grease and line an 18-cm round cake pan.

In a medium saucepan, combine the carrots, pears and pear juice. Simmer until the carrots and pears are very soft – about 10 minutes. Purée the carrots and pears, keeping all the juices. Add the butter and blend again until smooth. Into this, sift the flour and baking powder, and then stir in the polenta.

In a separate bowl, combine the eggs, lemon and lime zest, honey and vanilla essence. Stir this into the batter.

Spoon the batter into the prepared pan. Bake for 30–35 minutes, or until the centre of the cake springs back when lightly pressed. Let stand in the pan for a few minutes, then turn out onto a wire rack, remove the lining paper, and allow to cool.

To decorate, slice two pears lengthwise into thin slices and then drizzle with lemon juice. Sprinkle a baking tray with sugar, place the pear slices on the sugar and then sprinkle more sugar over the pears. Drizzle with more lemon juice. Dry in the oven for 30 minutes at 140 °C. Use to top the cake.

CARAMELIZED PEARS (OPTIONAL)
5 firm pears
4 cups (1 litre) water
juice of 1 lemon
1 cup (200 g) sugar
1 vanilla bean, split and scraped; retain seeds
150 g butter

Peel, quarter and core the pears. In a medium bowl, immerse the pears in the water and lemon juice.

In a large saucepan, combine the sugar, vanilla seeds and butter. Cook over low heat until the mixture becomes caramelized.

Dry the pears, and then add them to the caramel and cook until soft. Be sure to shake the saucepan frequently to prevent the pears from burning. Place the pears on the cake, drizzle with the remaining caramel and serve with whipped cream.

Raw Cake

At first we thought we were highly original when we created this recipe, but then we discovered that there are countless recipes for raw cake on the Internet! Nevertheless, we thoroughly enjoyed the process and will definitely create more of these fun recipes.

1 large watermelon

STRAWBERRY FILLING
1 avocado
1/2 cup (60 g) walnuts
1/2 cup (85 g) Calimyrna figs, soaked
1 cup (150 g) strawberries
1/2 cup (100 g) cooked beetroot pieces
1/2 cup (125 ml) coconut oil

Peel the avocado and discard the pip. Add it to a liquidizer along with the rest of the filling ingredients and blitz it all together until smooth. Refrigerate until set.

AVOCADO AND LIME FILLING
2 avocados
1/2 cup (60 g) macadamia nuts
1/2 cup (125 ml) coconut oil
2 Tbsp (30 ml) honey
1/2 cup (85 g) Calimyrna figs, soaked
zest and juice of 1 lime

Peel and slice the avocados; discard the pips. Add the avocados to a liquidizer along with the rest of the filling ingredients and blitz it all together until smooth. Refrigerate until set.

To assemble, slice the watermelon into thin rounds. Alternately layer watermelon slices with one of the fillings. Serve immediately.

Avocado and Sweet Potato Cake

We almost called this the 'Freaky Fuerte' after the cultivar of the much-loved avocado tree in our garden. Who knew you could have your veggies in your cake? Very moist, with a similar texture to that of a carrot cake.

1¹/₃ cups (235 g) brown sugar
125 g butter, softened
2 eggs
1 cup puréed avocado (2–3 avocados)
1 cup grated sweet potato (1 large, or 2 medium)
¹/₂ cup (60 g) chopped dates
¹/₂ cup (60 g) nuts of choice, chopped
1¹/₂ cups (210 g) flour
1¹/₂ tsp (7.5 ml) baking soda
1 tsp (5 ml) ground cinnamon
¹/₂ tsp (2.5 ml) ground nutmeg
¹/₄ tsp (1.25 ml) ground allspice
¹/₃ cup (80 ml) buttermilk

Preheat the oven to 180 °C. Grease and line a 23-cm square pan or a Bundt pan. In the mixing bowl of an electric mixer, fitted with a paddle attachment, cream the sugar and butter together. Add the eggs, one at a time, scraping down the sides of the bowl regularly. Add the avocado, sweet potato, dates and nuts. Sift the flour, baking soda and spices into the bowl. Stir in the buttermilk. Pour the mixture into the prepared pan and bake for 50–60 minutes. Cool in pan for 15 minutes before turning out. Cool completely before topping with Avocado Cream.

AVOCADO CREAM
1 cup (250 ml) cream
zest of 1 lime
1 avocado, puréed

In the bowl of an electric mixer, with a whisk attachment, whip the cream and lime zest together until stiff peak stage. Fold in the avocado purée.

Global
Superstars

Red Velvet Cake

SEXY! LUSCIOUS! **SIMPLY GORGEOUS!**

Something about this cake, our best-seller at Cakebread, compels us to spout adjectives! Perfect for Valentine's Day and weddings, as somehow it exudes love. We had our first bite in Charleston, South Carolina, and were immediately smitten. After some serious soul-searching we decided it would be rude not to part with our recipe. Still, it hurts! Dead easy to make, you can either bake 24 cupcakes, a three-layer 18-cm cake or a 23-cm single layer cake from this recipe. Simply double the recipe for a wedding cake or for larger batches.

2¹/₂ cups (350 g) flour
1¹/₂ cups (300 g) sugar
1 tsp (5 ml) bicarbonate of soda
1 tsp (5 ml) cocoa powder
1 tsp (5 ml) salt
1 cup (250 ml) buttermilk
2 eggs, at room temperature
1¹/₂ cups (375 ml) vegetable oil
1 tsp (5 ml) white vinegar
5 tsp (25 ml) red food colouring or a beetroot reduction
1 tsp (5 ml) vanilla essence
1 x quantity Cream Cheese Icing (see page 31)

Preheat the oven to 180 °C. Prepare your choice of baking pan, as mentioned above. (We used 3 x 18-cm cake pans for this one.)

In a large mixing bowl sift the flour, sugar, bicarbonate of soda, cocoa powder and salt together.

In another mixing bowl combine the buttermilk, eggs, oil, vinegar, food colouring and vanilla essence.

Mix the flour mixture into the buttermilk mixture. Pour the batter into the prepared pan and bake for 35–40 minutes for a large cake, and 18–20 minutes for cupcakes. Decorate with Cream Cheese Icing and organic rose petals.

Bahamian Rum Cake

Both of us called the Bahamas home on separate occasions and it is just as impossible not to fall in love with this moist, rich, nutty cake, as it is with the cool, clear water and swaying palm trees. The generous quantity of rum provides not only deep flavour, but acts as a preservative, allowing tourists to take away a bit of paradise in a tin. While it potentially lasts a long time, we've never made one that was not devoured on day one.

2^1/$_4$ cups (315 g) flour
1^1/$_3$ cups (270 g) sugar
1 Tbsp (15 ml) baking powder
^{1}/$_4$ tsp (1.25 ml) salt
110 g butter, melted
1 cup (250 ml) milk
^{1}/$_4$ cup (65 ml) rum
2 eggs, lightly beaten
1 tsp (5 ml) vanilla essence
1 cup (120 g) mixed nuts (we prefer macadamias and pecans)

RUM SAUCE
125 g butter
1 cup (200 g) sugar
^{1}/$_4$ cup (65 ml) water
^{1}/$_2$ cup (125 ml) rum

In a small saucepan, melt the butter and sugar in the water. Bring to the boil, remove from the heat and add the rum. Pour over the hot cake.

Preheat the oven to 180 °C. Grease a Bundt or a ring pan. Sift the flour, sugar, baking powder and salt together. In the bowl of an electric mixer, with the paddle attachment, mix the butter, milk, rum and eggs together. Add the flour mixture and beat until the batter is thoroughly mixed. Stir in the vanilla essence and nuts.

Pour the batter into the prepared pan and bake for 30–40 minutes, or until the middle springs back when lightly pressed. Pour the hot sauce over the cake, let it soak in completely, and then turn out.

Lemon, Lime and Coconut Cake

Driving over Lemons *is the title of one of our favourite novels. It centres around the trials and tribulations of an English couple who buy a farm in Andalusia, Spain. Callie sent me a copy while I was living in the Caribbean, where coconut and lime trees abound. Hence the pairing of lemon, lime and coconut.*

250 g butter
2 tsp (10 ml) lemon zest
2 cups (400 g) castor sugar
6 eggs
2 cups (280 g) flour, sifted
¼ cup (65 ml) self-raising flour, sifted
1 cup (250 ml) sour cream
1 cup (100 g) desiccated coconut, toasted

Preheat the oven to 180 °C. Grease and line 3 x 18-cm round cake pans. In the bowl of an electric mixer, with the paddle attachment, cream the butter, lemon zest and castor sugar until light and creamy. Add the eggs, one at a time, scraping down the sides of the bowl regularly. Alternately add the flours and the sour cream, starting and ending with the flour.

Spoon the batter into the prepared pans and bake for 1½ hours, or until the centre of the cake springs back when lightly pressed. Turn out onto a wire rack to cool.

Sandwich the layers with the Coconut Icing and ice the top and sides. Sprinkle all over with the coconut.

COCONUT ICING
1 cup (250 ml) cream
1 cup (250 g) mascarpone cheese
½ cup (125 ml) coconut cream
2 Tbsp (30 ml) icing sugar
zest from 1 lemon
zest from 1 lime

In the bowl of an electric mixer, with the whisk attachment, beat the cream until stiff peaks form.

In another bowl, combine the mascarpone cheese, coconut cream, icing sugar and the lemon and lime zests. Fold the whipped cream into this mixture.

Capri Cake

We were on our way to Turkey on a yacht when rough weather forced us to seek land for a few days. Upon docking at the island of Capri, our yacht was welcomed with the most delicious chocolate cake packaged in a beautiful wooden box. They call it a 'torta di ciccolato caprese'. After bumping my way round the galley for two rough days at sea, I was delighted not to have to conjure up anything myself and immediately served it to a delighted crew. – Mari-Louis

175 g dark chocolate
4 eggs, separated
³/₄ cup (150 g) castor sugar
1 tsp (5 ml) vanilla essence
1¹/₄ cups (125 g) ground almonds (almond flour)
175 g butter, melted
cocoa powder for dusting

Preheat the oven to 180 °C. Grease the sides of a 23-cm spring form cake pan and line the bottom with baking paper.

Finely chop the chocolate, but retain some texture.

In a mixing bowl, beat the egg yolks and castor sugar until pale and thick. Stir in the vanilla essence. Fold in the chocolate, almonds and melted butter. Set aside.

In another mixing bowl, beat the egg whites until soft peaks form. Fold the beaten egg white into the chocolate mixture. Spoon the batter into the prepared pan and bake for 50–60 minutes, or until just firm to the touch. Leave to cool before turning out. Dust with cocoa powder and serve with frozen cherries.

Boston Cream Pie

My absolute all-time favourite best best best best cake. It combines my three favourite C's: Cake, Chocolate and Custard. – Mari-Louis

1 cup (140 g) flour
2 tsp (10 ml) baking powder
pinch of salt
2 eggs, at room temperature
1 cup (200 g) sugar
1 tsp (5 ml) vanilla essence
1/2 cup (125 ml) milk
60 g butter

Preheat the oven to 180 °C. Grease and line 2 x 18-cm cake pans.
In a mixing bowl, sift the flour, baking powder and salt.
In another bowl, whisk the eggs and sugar until pale yellow.
Add the flour mixture to the egg mixture, and then stir in the vanilla essence.
In a small saucepan, bring the milk and the butter to the boil, then slowly add this to the batter, stirring gently.
Pour the batter into the prepared pans and bake for 25–30 minutes, or until the centre of the cake springs back when lightly pressed. Turn out onto wire racks and cool completely.
Spread the custard over one sponge. Refrigerate to set.
Top with the other sponge, and then pour the chocolate glaze over the assembled cake. Allow to set in the refrigerator before serving – about 30 minutes.

PASTRY CREAM (CUSTARD)
1 vanilla bean, split and scraped; seeds retained
2 cups (500 ml) milk
6 egg yolks
1/2 cup (100 g) castor sugar
1/4 cup (35 g) flour

In a saucepan, combine the vanilla seeds and milk. Bring to a boil.
In a mixing bowl, mix the yolks, sugar and flour. Bring the milk back to the boil and pour over the egg yolk mixture. Mix and strain into a clean pan. Bring to the boil, stirring continuously until thick – cook for a further 2 minutes. Pour into a bowl placed over ice.

CHOCOLATE GLAZE
100 g dark chocolate, chopped
1/2 cup (125 ml) cream

In a double boiler, melt the chocolate into the cream. Let cool until it reaches pouring consistency. Pour over the cake and decorate with coloured lustre dust (available at all cake shops – optional).

Mississippi Mud Cake

When I first came across this, the densest of all cakes, I thought the idea fairly strange. Then I discovered that it contains a good splash of bourbon, that most golden of American tipples. As they say in the States: Oh boy! I was instantly sold. Whether it is good old Jack Daniels, my friend Jim Beam, my Old Grand-Dad or that Wild Turkey, the result is a rich, satisfying, full flavour. – Callie

250 g butter, cut into blocks
200 g dark chocolate, chopped
2 cups (400 g) sugar
1 cup (250 ml) milk
1 tsp (5 ml) vanilla essence
¹/₃ cup (80 ml) bourbon
1³/₄ cup (245 g) flour
1 tsp (5 ml) baking powder
¹/₄ cup (30 g) cocoa powder
2 eggs, lightly beaten

Preheat the oven to 180 °C. Grease and line a deep 20-cm square cake pan or 2 x 23-cm loaf pans.

In a medium saucepan, combine the butter, chocolate, sugar, milk, vanilla essence and bourbon. Stir over low heat until smooth. Remove from the heat and cool for 10 minutes.

Pour into a large mixing bowl, sift in the flour, baking powder and cocoa powder. Stir in the eggs until well combined. Pour the batter into the prepared pan and bake for 1¹/₄ hours (45–55 minutes for the loaf pans), or until the centre of the cake is firm to the touch.

Let it cool in the pan for 15 minutes before turning out. Decorate with dark chocolate Bourbon Ganache.

BOURBON GANACHE
200 g best quality dark chocolate
¹/₃ cup (80 ml) cream
2 Tbsp (30 ml) bourbon

Chop the chocolate into pieces. In a double boiler, combine the cream with the chocolate. Stir until smooth. Remove from heat, and then stir in the bourbon. Cool until the mixture is spreadable.

Concorde Cake

Named by a Parisian chef in celebration of the supersonic passenger jet, the Concorde is an all-chocolate layered dessert. We have the beautiful Mrs O. from Lyford Cay to thank for the lovely mousse filling. At the Cakebread bakery we also do a strawberry, vanilla and white chocolate version.

1 cup (140 g) icing sugar
6 Tbsp (90 ml) cocoa powder
5 egg whites
¾ cup (150 g) castor sugar
1 tsp (5 ml) vanilla essence
icing sugar for dusting

Preheat the oven to 110 °C.

Line 2 large baking trays with baking paper.

In a medium bowl, sift the icing sugar and cocoa powder together.

In the bowl of an electric mixer, with the whisk attachment, beat the egg whites until soft peaks form. Gradually beat in the castor sugar and continue beating until stiff peaks form and the meringue is glossy and smooth. Fold in the icing sugar and cocoa mixture, as well as the vanilla essence.

On one of the baking trays, draw a 23-cm diameter circle on the baking paper. Spread some of the meringue mix inside this circle to form a large round; this will later form the base for the cake. Fit a piping bag with a large plain nozzle. On the second baking tray, pipe long strips of meringue, leaving at least 2.5 cm between the strips. Bake for at least 2 hours, until the meringue is crisp and dry. Cool, peel off the paper, and then set aside.

To assemble: Using a spatula, spread the chocolate mousse over the meringue round. Cut the meringue strips into desired lengths with a serrated knife, and use them to decorate the top and sides of the cake. Sift icing sugar over the top. Cover and refrigerate for 2 hours before serving.

CHOCOLATE MOUSSE

300 g dark chocolate
2 Tbsp (30 ml) espresso
2 Tbsp (30 ml) cognac or brandy
6 eggs, separated
¾ cup (150 g) sugar
170 g soft butter

In a double boiler, melt the chocolate in the espresso. Stir in the cognac. Set aside.

In the bowl of an electric mixer, with the paddle attachment, beat the egg yolks with the sugar until pale and ribbony. Add the chocolate mixture to the egg mixture. Gradually beat in spoonfuls of the soft butter.

In another mixing bowl, beat the egg whites until stiff peak stage. Fold the egg whites into the chocolate mixture. Cool until slightly set.

BAKER'S SECRET: For foolproof results use a Silpad instead of baking paper.

Russian Tea Cake

Our grandmother worked as an au pair for a Jewish family and this was one of her treasured recipes. In many ways she was a truly remarkable woman; she married at the then ripe old age of 26 and well into her eighties she was still very interested in all things new and wonderful. She loved the fact that we loved travelling and made certain she read up on the beautiful places we visited. This is a very Afrikaans version of an old classic. This cake is best made several hours before eating as the layers become lovely and moist as the cake ages.

4 cups (560 g) flour
1 tsp (5ml) salt
2 tsp (10 ml) baking powder
1 cup (200 g) sugar
250 g butter
3 eggs, beaten
ground cinnamon or cake crumbs for dusting

CUSTARD FILLING
2 cups (500 ml) steeped rooibos tea
1 cup (250 ml) milk
3 Tbsp (45 ml) custard powder
3 Tbsp (45 ml) cornflour
³/₄ cup (150 g) sugar
1 egg, beaten
1 Tbsp (15 ml) vanilla essence

Preheat the oven to 180 °C.
Grease and line 2 x 22-cm cake pans.
Into the bowl of an electric mixer, with the paddle attachment, sift the flour, salt and baking powder together.
Add the sugar and butter and mix to a breadcrumb consistency.
Add the eggs, one at a time, while beating slowly, until a paste forms. Form the paste into a disk.
Shape and place in the refrigerator for 30 minutes.
Divide the dough into eight parts (140 g each). Roll out two pieces at a time to line the bottom of the pans. Use baking paper rounds to make sure the dough fits. Bake for 20 minutes, until golden brown. Repeat until all eight rounds are baked.
To assemble, divide the custard into eight parts. Spread the custard over each layer and stack each layer on top of the other.
Sprinkle with ground cinnamon or cake crumbs.

In a medium saucepan, heat the tea and milk together. Remove from the heat. Set aside.

In a medium bowl, sift the custard powder, cornflour and sugar together. Add the egg and stir until it becomes a dry paste. In a steady stream, add the milky tea. Return this mixture to the saucepan, stirring over medium heat until it thickens. Remove from the heat and stir in the vanilla essence. Cool.

Fresh Fruit

Chocolate Strawberry Cake

Take an easy chocolate cake recipe, bake in a differently shaped pan, pair it with some beautiful strawberries and voilà! ... an elegant cake that would have made Marie Antoinette proud.

2 cups (400 g) sugar
1³/₄ cups (245 g) flour
³/₄ cup (90 g) cocoa powder
1¹/₂ tsp (7.5 ml) baking powder
1¹/₂ tsp (7.5 ml) bicarbonate of soda
1 tsp (5 ml) salt
2 eggs, at room temperature
1 cup (250 ml) milk
¹/₂ cup (125 ml) vegetable oil
2 tsp (10 ml) vanilla essence
1 cup (250 ml) boiling water
3 cups (about 465 g) fresh strawberries
1 Tbsp (15 ml) strawberry jam

CHOCOLATE GANACHE
200 g best quality dark chocolate
¹/₃ cup (80 ml) cream

Chop the chocolate into pieces. In a double boiler, combine the cream with the chocolate. Stir until smooth. Remove from heat and cool slightly

Preheat the oven to 180 °C. Grease and line a 23-cm loaf pan. Sift the sugar, flour, cocoa, baking powder, bicarbonate of soda and salt into the bowl of an electric mixer fitted with the paddle attachment. Add the eggs, milk, oil and vanilla essence. Beat for 2 minutes on medium speed.

Stir in the boiling water. The batter should be runny. Pour the batter into the prepared pan, and then bake for 30–35 minutes, or until the centre of the cake springs back when lightly pressed.

Cool in the pan for at least 10 minutes, then turn out. Pour the chocolate ganache over the cake. Cut the tops off the strawberries and arrange end up on the cake. Melt the jam for a few seconds in a microwave. Brush the jam onto the strawberries for that extra sheen.

Ginger and Quince Preserve Cake

Quince has always been a magical fruit for us. To see this pale, humble-looking fruit change colour to soft rose-pink and then deep red when baked or poached is still wonderful to behold. In our travels to Argentina we were delighted to see that they use this fruit as often as we do. This cake is also lovely if you exchange the quince with poached pears.

SYRUP

3 cups (750 ml) water
³/₄ cup (150 g) sugar
1 cinnamon stick
1 star anise
juice of 1 lemon
3 quinces

In a large saucepan over low heat, stir the water, sugar, cinnamon, star anise and lemon juice together. Add the quinces and bring to the boil. Reduce the heat and simmer for 1¹/₂ hours, or until the quinces turn a light pink. Should you wish for a darker colour, add a drop of red food colouring or beetroot juice. Cool the quinces in the syrup to room temperature. Chop 1 quince into small pieces and reserve the remaining quinces (sliced) and the syrup for decoration.

CAKE

250 g butter, chopped
²/₃ cup (160 ml) golden syrup
60 g preserved ginger, chopped (or Japanese pickled ginger)
1 cup (140 g) flour
1 cup (140 g) self-raising flour
³/₄ cup (190 ml) cream
2 eggs
chopped cooked quince (see Syrup)
¹/₂ tsp (2.5 ml) bicarbonate of soda

Preheat the oven to 180 °C. Grease a deep 22-cm square pan, and line the base and sides with baking paper.

In a medium saucepan, melt the butter and golden syrup together. Remove from the heat and stir in the ginger.

In a mixing bowl, sift the flours together. Set aside.

In a large mixing bowl, combine the syrup mixture with the cream, eggs, chopped quince and bicarbonate of soda. Fold in the flour. Pour the batter into the prepared pan, and then bake for 40 minutes, or until the centre of the cake springs back when lightly pressed.

While the cake is still hot, drench it with the reserved syrup before turning out and decorating with the reserved quinces. Serve warm with double-thick cream.

Banana Butterscotch

My first ever memory of baking saw our dad, Mari-Louis and myself get totally carried away with the first ripe bunch of bananas from our garden. Without our mother there to give guidance or preach temperance, we soon ran out of cake and bread pans as we grabbed anything remotely hollow and heat resistant. We ended up with nine cakes, each a different size and shape! – Callie

3 eggs

2 cups (400 g) sugar

1¹/₃ cups (330 ml) vegetable oil

3 ripe bananas, mashed

¹/₃ cup (80 ml) buttermilk or sour cream

1 Tbsp (15 ml) vanilla essence

3 cups (420 g) flour

1 tsp (5 ml) baking powder

pinch of salt

¹/₄ cup (25 g) desiccated coconut

¹/₂ cup (60 g) walnuts

Preheat the oven to 180 °C. Grease two medium loaf pans and line the bottoms with baking paper.

In a large bowl, whisk together the eggs, sugar, oil, bananas, buttermilk or sour cream, and vanilla essence. Set aside.

In another bowl, sift together the flour, baking powder and salt. Add this to the wet mixture, and then stir in the coconut and walnuts. Pour the batter into the prepared pans, and then bake for 30–40 minutes, or until a skewer comes out clean.

As soon as the cakes come out of the oven, pierce them all over with a skewer and pour the bubbling butterscotch over the top. Leave to cool in the pan.

BUTTERSCOTCH

¹/₂ cup (100 g) soft brown sugar

70 g unsalted butter

4 Tbsp (60 ml) cream

Place all the ingredients in a saucepan and heat gently until the sugar has dissolved and the mixture is bubbling.

Summer Berry Cake

'All I ask is that you treat me like you would Martha!' (Slogan on an apron that Callie gave me.)

Definitely inspired by Martha Stewart, this simple stunner is our Vanilla Hot Milk Sponge, to which you can add your favourite topping.
– Mari-Louis

2 cups (280 g) flour	**BERRY FILLING/TOPPING**
1 Tbsp (15 ml) baking powder	**4 cups (1 litre) cream**
pinch of salt	**1/2 cup (70 g) icing sugar**
4 eggs, at room temperature	**1 tsp (5 ml) vanilla essence**
2 cups (400 g) sugar	**3 cups mixed berries in season (blueberries, strawberries,**
1 tsp (5 ml) vanilla essence	**raspberries, gooseberries)**
120 g butter	
1 cup (250 ml) milk	

Preheat the oven to 180 °C. Grease and line 2 x 18-cm round pans or 4 shallow heart-shaped pans.

In a mixing bowl, sift the flour, baking powder and salt.

In another bowl, whisk the eggs and sugar until pale yellow. Add the flour mixture to the egg mixture, and then stir in the vanilla.

In a small saucepan, bring the butter and milk to the boil, then slowly add this to the batter, stirring gently. Pour the batter into the prepared pans and bake for 25–30 minutes for the 18-cm pans, or 20–25 minutes for the heart-shaped pans, or until the centre of the cake springs back when lightly pressed. Turn out onto wire racks to cool.

To make the filling/topping, in the bowl of an electric mixer with the whisk attachment, combine the cream, icing sugar and vanilla essence. Gradually increase the speed until stiff peaks form.

For round cakes, split each cake into two layers. Spread each layer with cream and scatter with berries. Repeat for all four layers.

Mango Mess Cake

We can never wait for these lush, tropical babies to come into season. Then it is off to a quiet corner, because face it, this is not normally a fruit to be eaten in public. Part of the joy of a mango is to get completely messy, juice running down your cheeks and fibres sticking out from your front teeth! Truly, for us, the smell of summer.

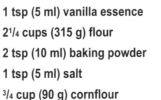

225 g butter
1¾ cups (350 g) castor sugar
4 eggs, at room temperature

1 tsp (5 ml) vanilla essence
2¼ cups (315 g) flour
2 tsp (10 ml) baking powder
1 tsp (5 ml) salt
¾ cup (90 g) cornflour
1 cup (250 ml) evaporated milk
1 x 400 g can mangoes, chopped (reserve the juice)

Preheat the oven to 180 °C. Grease and line 2 x18-cm ring pans or 1 large sheet pan.

In a large mixing bowl, cream the butter and castor sugar until light in colour. Add the eggs, one at a time, beating well after each addition. Add the vanilla essence and incorporate.

In a separate bowl, sift the flour, baking powder, salt and cornflour together. Alternately add the flour mixture and the evaporated milk to the butter mixture, starting and ending with the flour. Stir in the mangoes until combined.

Spoon the batter into the prepared pans and bake for 35–40 minutes, or until the centre of the cake springs back when lightly pressed. Drizzle with the reserved mango juice and let it cool in the pan before turning out. Spread generous amounts of Mango Cream between the layers and/or on top.

MANGO CREAM
1 cup (250 ml) cream
1 mango, sliced
4 small meringues, broken into pieces

Beat the cream until stiff peaks form. Fold in the mango slices and broken meringue.

Peach Jelly Roll

On a Spanish holiday with my husband, Chris, we were enjoying tapas in some small town where we met a man who had relocated there from Upington in the Northern Cape of South Africa some 20 years before. He did not quite believe that we were from South Africa until he had us say 'peaches and cream'. Apparently this phrase was sure to give away our native accent. This cake is a creation borne from that incident.

2 Tbsp (30 ml) castor sugar
6 large eggs, separated
3/4 cup (150 g) castor sugar
1/2 cup (70 g) flour
3 Tbsp (45 ml) smooth peach jam
1 cup (250 ml) cream, whipped
4 fresh peaches, sliced

SECRET: Heat the jam in the microwave for a few seconds to make spreading easier.

Preheat the oven to 170 °C. Line a swiss roll pan with baking paper, ensuring that you grease the sides. Dust a clean dishcloth with the 2 Tbsp castor sugar.

Using an electric mixer with a whisk attachment, beat the egg yolks until thick and very pale. Transfer to another bowl and set aside.

In a clean bowl, with the whisk attachment, beat the egg whites until foamy. Increase the speed and gradually add the castor sugar. Beat on high speed until stiff peaks form. Sift the flour into the mixture. Fold in until just combined. Gently fold in the egg yolks. Spoon the batter into the prepared pan, ensuring that it spreads into the corners. Bake for 15 minutes, or until the centre of the cake springs back when gently touched. Immediately turn the cake out onto the dusted dishcloth. Carefully peel off the baking paper, spread with the jam and roll the cake up lengthwise using the cloth to help. Leave to cool completely.

When cooled, roll out again and fill with cream and peach slices. Carefully roll up again and serve.

Passion Fruit Cake

To us at Cakebread this recipe epitomizes how simplicity can sometimes be so much more appealing than overly elaborate cakes. The relationship between the lime and passion fruit is divine. It also gives us an excuse to use our older cake pans with unusual shapes.

250 g butter
2 cups (400 g) castor sugar
6 eggs
2 cups (280 g) flour
1/4 cup (35 g) self-raising flour
1 cup (250 ml) sour cream
zest of 2 limes

Preheat the oven to 180 °C.

Grease and line a 27-cm round cake pan or a Bundt pan. In the bowl of an electric mixer, with the paddle attachment, cream the butter and castor sugar until light and creamy. Add the eggs, one at a time, scraping down the sides of the bowl regularly. In a separate bowl, sift the flours together. Add half of the flour mixture to the sugar mixture, followed by the sour cream and then the last of the flour. Stir in the zest.

Spoon the batter into the prepared pan, and then bake for 1 1/2 hours, or until the centre of the cake springs back when lightly pressed. Remove from oven and rest for 10 minutes. Remove the cake from the pan and place on a serving plate. Spike all over with a thin skewer, drizzle the cake with Passion Fruit Syrup and serve while still warm. For special occasions, serve with Passion Fruit Curd.

PASSION FRUIT SYRUP
1 cup (250 ml) passion fruit (granadilla) pulp
1/2 cup (125 ml) water
1/2 cup (100 g) sugar

In a medium saucepan over medium heat, combine the passion fruit pulp, water and sugar. Stir until the sugar has dissolved, then bring to the boil. Reduce the heat and simmer uncovered for 10–12 minutes, or until syrupy.

PASSION FRUIT CURD
8 large egg yolks
1 cup (250 ml) passion fruit (granadilla) pulp
1 cup (200 g) sugar
pinch of salt
150 g cold butter, diced

In a bowl over a pan of simmering water, add the egg yolks, passion fruit pulp and sugar and salt. Stir with a wooden spoon for 8–10 minutes until thick. Remove from the heat and whisk in the butter. Cool completely before using, or keep for up to a month in small pots.

High Days
and Holy Days

Strawberry Cake

If Barbie ate cake … This fun cake is great for those super-fun girlie events, like sweet sixteens and hen parties.

30 g butter
1¼ cups (250 g) sugar
4 eggs, at room temperature
2 cups (280 g) self-raising flour
⅓ cup (80 g) strawberry jelly powder
1 cup (250 ml) milk
strawberries to decorate

Preheat the oven to 180 °C. Grease 2 x 18-cm round cake pans. In the bowl of an electric mixer, with a paddle attachment, beat the butter and sugar until light and fluffy. Add the eggs, one at a time, scraping down the sides of the bowl regularly. Add the flour, jelly powder and milk. Beat until well combined.
Spoon the mixture into the prepared pans, and then bake for 35–40 minutes, or until the centre of the cake springs back when lightly pressed. Turn out onto a rack to cool.
Sandwich the cake layers together with some of the buttercream and strawberries, and then ice the cake all around with the remaining buttercream. Decorate with fresh strawberries.

STRAWBERRY BUTTERCREAM ICING
125 g butter, softened
1½ cups (210 g) icing sugar, sifted
2 Tbsp (30 ml) milk
1 tsp (5 ml) strawberry essence
pink food colouring (a little goes a long way)

In the bowl of an electric mixer, with the paddle attachment, beat the butter until pale and creamy. Add the icing sugar and half of the milk. Beat until combined. Add the strawberry essence and food colouring as required. If the mixture is too firm, add the rest of the milk and beat until you achieve the desired consistency.

Yule Log

Chocolate cake, chocolate mousse, chocolate butter cream. We love the French for being different from the rest of the world. Instead of fruit cake, they use this trio of decadent chocolate to get into a festive mood.

5 eggs, separated
140 g castor sugar
75 g self-raising flour
¹/₃ cup (40 g) cocoa powder
castor sugar for sprinkling
1 x quantity Chocolate Mousse (see page 82)
chocolate leaves and icing sugar to decorate

Preheat the oven to 180 °C. Grease and line a 23 x 32 cm baking tray. In the bowl of an electric mixer, with a whisk attachment, whisk the egg yolks with the 140 g castor sugar until light and ribbony. Sift the flour and cocoa powder into the mixing bowl, and then fold in gently until thoroughly combined.

In a clean mixing bowl, whisk the egg whites until stiff peak stage. Fold into the cocoa batter. Spoon the batter into the prepared tray, and then bake for 10–15 minutes, or until the top is firm to the touch.

Place a piece of baking paper slightly larger than a dishcloth over a large dishcloth and sprinkle liberally with castor sugar. Turn out the baked sponge onto the dishcloth and gently, with the help of the cloth, roll up. Leave it to rest with the dishcloth still around it for 20–30 minutes, or until the roll is completely cool.

To assemble, unroll the sponge and remove the baking paper. Spread with the Chocolate Mousse, and then roll up again. Trim the sides to neaten roll. Decorate with Chocolate Buttercream Icing and Chocolate Leaves. Dust with icing sugar.

CHOCOLATE BUTTERCREAM ICING
250 g butter, softened
1¹/₃ cups (160 g) cocoa powder, sifted
5 cups (700 g) icing sugar, sifted
²/₃ cup (160 ml) milk
2 tsp (10 ml) vanilla essence

In the bowl of an electric mixer, with the paddle attachment, beat the butter and cocoa powder until combined. Add half of the icing sugar, followed by the milk and the rest of the icing sugar. Add the vanilla essence and beat until fluffy. Use this to pipe patterns to imitate tree bark onto the cake.

CHOCOLATE LEAVES: Pick and rinse a few handfuls of oak leaves. In a double-boiler, melt 200 g dark chocolate. Brush the melted chocolate on the underside of the leaves. Refrigerate to harden and then gently peel the leaves and the chocolate apart.

Traditional Fruit Cake

Try the home-made way for your wedding and Christmas cakes and fall in love again with this richest of cakes. The combination of the nuts, fruit and brandy leaves you with a cake that is moist and, if properly stored, just about keeps forever. We make ours three months in advance in order for the cake to mellow and flavour to develop, but a month ahead of time is plenty. Do not feel bound by the ingredients: if there are some you don't like, substitute the like amount of what you do like. Just about any glazed or dried fruit of your choice will do. Use wine if you prefer this to brandy or use citrus juice if you are a teetotaller. Grandma's recipe was a multi-day event, but at Cakebread we don't have that amount of time available, so our recipe speeds up the process to fit the modern baker.

3 cups (750 ml) water
3 cups (600 g) sugar
375 g butter
6 cups (1.5 kg) dried fruit and nut mix
1 cup (150 g) dates, chopped
1 cup (200 g) glazed cherries
1 Tbsp (15 ml) bicarbonate of soda
6 eggs, at room temperature
6 cups (840 g) flour
1 Tbsp (15 ml) baking powder
1 Tbsp (15 ml) ground cinnamon
1 tsp (5 ml) ground ginger
1 tsp (5 ml) ground cloves
1 tsp (5 ml) ground nutmeg
1 cup (250 ml) brandy

Preheat the oven to 180 °C. Line a 30-cm round or square pan (or 1 x 15-cm and 1 x 23-cm pan if you want to create a tiered cake).

In a large saucepan over medium heat, combine the water, sugar and butter. Stir until the sugar is dissolved and boil for 5 minutes. Remove from the heat and stir in the dried fruit, nuts, dates and cherries. Return to the heat and bring to a boil for 15 minutes. Remove from the heat and stir in the bicarbonate of soda until well combined. Set aside to cool completely.

Beat the eggs, and then stir them into the cooled mixture.

In a separate bowl, sift the flour, baking powder and spices together. Fold this mixture into the fruit mixture. Pour the batter evenly into the prepared pans, and then bake for 1 hour. Reduce oven temperature to 150 °C and bake for a further 1 hour for the large pan, 35–40 minutes for the 15-cm pan, or 45–50 minutes for the 23-cm pan. The tester should come out clean and moist, but not doughy, to show that the cake is done. Pour the brandy evenly over the cake and leave in the pan until the next day.

Covered in foil, this cake will stay fresh for a long, long time. It really does mature over time – we unwrap ours once a month and sprinkle with some more brandy.

For our mini fruit cakes, we baked them in dariole moulds (baking time 35 minutes), but you can just as easily press shapes out of your large cake.

Serve as is or cover with a thin layer of marzipan, followed by a layer of fondant (see page 109).

Easter Cupcakes

An excuse to add another cute cupcake to your repertoire. This is a no-fail recipe that is absolutely versatile to boot. For children's parties, substitute some of the liquid in the icing with carrot, beetroot or cranberry juice for different colours and flavours.

250 g butter, softened
1 cup (200 g) castor sugar
2 cups (280 g) self-raising flour, sifted
1 tsp (5 ml) baking powder, sifted
4 eggs
1 tsp (5 ml) vanilla essence

Preheat the oven to 180 °C.
Prepare muffin pans with 20 paper cups.
In the bowl of an electric mixer, with the paddle attachment,
beat all the ingredients together until smooth and pale, about
3 minutes. Spoon the mixture into the cups and bake for
20 minutes. Cool completely and then decorate with coloured
liquid fondant icing and top with Fondant Nests.

LIQUID FONDANT ICING
1 cup (140 g) icing sugar, sifted
5 tsp (25 ml) water
1 tsp (5 ml) liquid glucose
drop of colouring of choice

In a medium saucepan, combine the icing sugar, water and
glucose. Cook over a low heat, stirring continuously. Add the food
colouring. The mixture should be thin enough to pour, yet thick
enough to coat.

FONDANT NESTS

300 g ready-made fondant (also known as 'plastic icing')
brown food colouring

Colour the fondant (see page 106) and set aside for 5 minutes.
Push the fondant through a garlic press or pasta maker on
spaghetti setting. Form the resulting strands into a nest shape.
Fill the nest with chocolate eggs.

German Chocolate Cake

This cake is not German at all, but American! It was created by a housewife in 1957 using Baker's German's Sweet Chocolate. The apostrophe disappeared and it became a German chocolate cake. This is the authentic recipe. It is usually a three-layered cake and we have made it like that for weddings, but it is equally lovely as a sheet with the glorious topping. If you do decide to make a tiered cake, double the icing ingredients.

100 g sweet milk chocolate
1/2 cup (125 ml) water
2 cups (280 g) flour
1 tsp (5 ml) bicarbonate of soda
pinch of salt
250 g butter, softened
2 cups (400 g) sugar
4 eggs, separated
1 tsp (5 ml) vanilla essence
1 cup (250 ml) buttermilk
1 x quantity Chocolate Buttercream Icing (see page 104)

COCONUT-PECAN FILLING
4 egg yolks
11/4 cups (315 ml) evaporated milk
11/2 tsp (7.5 ml) vanilla essence
11/2 cups (300 g) sugar
190 g butter
2 cups (200 g) desiccated coconut
11/2 cups (180 g) pecan nuts, chopped and roasted

Preheat the oven to 180 °C. Grease and line 3 x 18-cm pans. In a large heatproof mixing bowl, microwave the chocolate and water for 11/2–2 minutes, stirring after 1 minute. Stir until the chocolate is completely melted. In a mixing bowl, sift the flour, bicarbonate of soda and salt together. Set aside. In the bowl of an electric mixer, with the paddle attachment, beat the butter and sugar until light and fluffy. Add the egg yolks, one at a time, scraping down the sides of the bowl regularly. Blend in the melted chocolate and vanilla essence. Add the flour mixture alternately with the buttermilk, beating well after each addition. In the bowl of an electric mixer, with the whisk attachment, whisk the egg whites until stiff peaks form. Gently stir this into the batter. Pour the batter into the prepared pans, and then bake for 30–35 minutes, or until the centre of the cake springs back when lightly pressed. Immediately run a small metal spatula around the edge of each layer. Cool in pans for 15 minutes, and then turn out onto a wire rack. Cool completely. Spread Coconut-Pecan Filling over each layer and stack the layers on top of each other. Ice with Chocolate Buttercream Icing.

In a large saucepan, combine the egg yolks, evaporated milk and vanilla essence and whisk until well blended. Add the sugar and butter. Cook on medium heat for 12 minutes, stirring constantly. Remove from the heat, and then add the coconut and pecan nuts. Mix well. Cool to a spreadable consistency.

TIP: If pressed for time, simply stir coconut into tinned caramel.

Bourbon Chocolate Cake

Mari-Louis spent some time learning fondant techniques from master craftswoman Colette Peters in New York. She handed down this recipe that she uses for her wedding cakes, and which we use as a base for many of ours. This recipe can be doubled for larger cakes.

2 cups (280 g) flour
1 tsp (5 ml) bicarbonate of soda
pinch of salt
1³/₄ cups (440 ml) hot black coffee
¹/₄ cup (65 ml) bourbon
250 g butter, cut into small pieces
125 g unsweetened chocolate, cut into small pieces
2 cups (400 g) sugar
2 eggs, at room temperature
1 tsp (5 ml) vanilla essence

NOTE: To make this three-tier wedding cake, you will have to make the batter six times. Divide one quantity batter between the 18-cm pans, use one quantity batter for each of the 23-cm pans and use 1½ quantity batter for each of the 27.5-cm pans. You will also need a 30-cm cake stand, 3 x cake dividers (same size as layers), 5-mm dowels and a cake smoother.

Preheat the oven to 140 °C. Grease and flour 2 x 18-cm, 2 x 23-cm and 2 x 27.5-cm cake pans. Sift the flour, bicarbonate of soda and salt together. In a separate mixing bowl, combine the coffee, bourbon, butter and chocolate. Place over a double boiler and heat slowly, stirring constantly until the chocolate has melted. Whisk in the sugar and cool. Whisk in the flour mixture in two batches and then add the eggs and vanilla essence. Pour the batter into the pans and bake for 70 minutes, or until the centre springs back when slightly pressed. Leave in the pans until completely cooled. To remove the cakes, run a knife around the edges and place the pan over a low flame to melt the grease, making sure to keep the pan moving to prevent burning. The cake should slide out easily when inverted. Slice each cake into two layers and spread the butter-cream in between the layers. You should have four layers per tier.

CAPPUCCINO BUTTERCREAM ICING
225 g butter
450 g firm margarine
11½ cups (1.5 kg) icing sugar, sifted
1½ tsp (7.5 ml) vanilla essence
4 Tbsp (60 ml) coffee powder, dissolved in 1 Tbsp (15 ml) boiling water

Cream the butter and margarine until smooth. Add the icing sugar and vanilla essence and mix well. Add the coffee. Use 550 g buttercream for the 18-cm cakes, 700 g for the 23-cm cakes and 1 kg for the 27.5-cm cakes.

FONDANT (FOR THE CAKE)
2.5–3 kg fondant
cornflour
2–4 Tbsp (30–60 ml) tylose

Knead the fondant until slightly soft on a surface sprinkled with cornflour. Use 20 ml (4 tsp) tylose per kg of fondant and work it into the fondant thoroughly. Wrap in clingfilm and let it stand for 30 minutes.

FONDANT STRIPS (FOR DECORATING)
1–1.5 kg fondant
pink food colouring (powder or concentrated liquid)
brown food colouring (powder or concentrated liquid)

Prepare the fondant as above. Divide into four portions. Leave one portion white, and work brown and pink food colouring into the other three portions until you have the desired colours.

ROYAL ICING

1½ cups (210 g) icing sugar, sifted

1 egg white

Stir icing sugar into the egg white.

TO ASSEMBLE THE CAKE

Cut holes the size of a large coin through the centre of each divider before placing each layer onto the divider. Apply a 'crumb coat' of meringue icing over each layer (see recipe on page 114). Roll out a piece of fondant (on a smooth work surface dusted with cornflour) to about 3 mm thick and 1½ times the size of the layer you are about to cover. Lightly place the rolled fondant over the centre of the cake and immediately smooth down the sides. Where folds occur, gently lift the fondant and smooth out again. Cut off the excess fondant and use the cake paddle to smooth the cake even more. Tuck the edges in neatly under the cake. Proceed to cover the other two cakes. Leave overnight to harden.

Place a little Royal Icing (see page 113) on the cake stand before the bottom tier is placed on it to prevent the cake from sliding around. Cut four dowels the height of the bottom tier and insert in a square around the centre to support the second tier. Repeat for the third tier, but do not insert dowels into the top. Insert a dowel the height of the entire cake down the centre, through the holes in the dividers. Fill the gaps between the tiers with Royal Icing. Roll out the fondant you will use for the strips. Cut 1.5 cm strips that will be long enough to go around the cake.

Start with the bottom tier. Brush it with glue. Roll up a bright pink strip very loosely and unroll onto the cake pressing it lightly in place. Cut off the extra piece. Brush the top rim with glue where the second strip will overlap slightly. Add the strips in the following pattern: Bright pink, brown, bright pink, white, light pink and repeat the pattern. Decorate the cake with a fresh or a sugar rose.

NOTE: To make confectioner's glue, add 200 ml cold water to 2 Tbsp (30 ml) tylose. Stir until all lumps are gone. Let it stand for 30 minutes to thicken. It should have the consistency of honey. If it gets too thick, just add more water.

White Wedding Cake

Another one from Colette Peters, the most jovial, fun cake maker who keeps the rest of us on our toes with her constant reinventing of the sugar craft. This cake can be flavoured with a dash of your choice of liqueur.

125 g butter
1½ cups (300 g) sugar
2 tsp (10 ml) vanilla essence
2¾ cups (385 g) flour
4 tsp (20 ml) baking powder
½ tsp (2.5 ml) salt
1 cup (250 ml) milk
4 egg whites

NOTE: To make this three-tier wedding cake, you'll have to make the batter six times. Divide one quantity between the 18-cm pans, use one quantity for each of the 23-cm pans and use 1½ quantity for each of the 27.5-cm pans. You'll also need a 30-cm cake stand, 3 x cake dividers (same size as layers), 5-mm dowels, a cake smoother, small paint brush, 2.3-cm and 3-cm round cutters

Preheat the oven to 180 °C. Grease and flour 2 x 18-cm, 2 x 23 cm and 2 x 27.5cm cake pans. Cream the butter until light and airy. Slowly add 1 cup (200 g) sugar while constantly beating until light and fluffy. Add the vanilla essence. In a small bowl, sift the flour, baking powder and salt together. Add the flour and milk alternately to the butter mixture, starting and ending with the flour. In a clean bowl, whisk the egg whites until fluffy. Slowly add the remaining sugar and whisk until stiff and shiny peaks form. Gently fold the egg white mixture into the batter until blended; don't overmix. Pour the batter into the prepared pans and bake for 50–60 minutes, or until the centre springs back when lightly pressed. Cool the cakes on a wire rack for 15 minutes before turning out. Cool completely, then wrap and refrigerate before decorating. Slice each cake into two layers and spread the Raspberry Buttercream Icing between the layers. You should have four layers per tier. Spread each cake with the Meringue Icing.

RASPBERRY COULIS
250 g raspberries
4 Tbsp (60 ml) water
½ cup (100 g) sugar

Combine the raspberries, water and sugar in a pot. Cook slowly until the raspberries disintegrate and the coulis has thickened.

RASPBERRY BUTTERCREAM ICING
225 g butter
450 g firm margarine
11½ cups (1.5 kg) icing sugar, sifted
1½ tsp (7.5 ml) vanilla essence
red food colouring

Cream the butter and margarine until smooth. Add the icing sugar and the vanilla essence and mix well. Stir in the raspberry coulis. If the colour is not pink enough, add a few drops of food colouring.
Use 550 g buttercream for the 18-cm cakes, 700 g for the 23-cm cakes and 1.1 kg for the 27.5-cm cakes.

MERINGUE ICING
4 egg whites
1 cup (200 g) sugar

Place the egg whites and sugar over a double boiler and whisk constantly until the mixture is white, glossy and hot to the touch. Place the mixture in a mixing bowl and beat well for 7 minutes until it is very stiff and glossy.

FONDANT (FOR THE CAKE)
Use same recipe as on page 112.

FONDANT CIRCLES (FOR DECORATING)
1 kg fondant
cornflour
4 tsp (20 ml) tylose
clear alcohol or lemon essence
silver food colouring (powder)

Prepare the fondant as described on page 112. To make the circles, roll out 500 g of treated fondant. Cut circles with the 3-cm cutter and then cut out the centre with the smaller cutter. Once dry, paint the circles silver by adding a little alcohol to the silver powder. Only make the white circles when you are ready to assemble the cake because they still need to be soft so that they can be placed on the curves of the cake without breaking.

TO ASSEMBLE THE CAKE
Cut holes the size of a large coin through the centre of each divider before placing each layer onto the divider. Apply a 'crumb coat' of meringue icing over each layer. Roll out a piece of fondant (on a smooth work surface dusted with cornflour) to about 3 mm thick and 1½ times the size of the layer you are about to cover. Lightly place the rolled fondant over the centre of the cake and immediately smooth down the sides. Where folds occur, gently lift the fondant and smooth out again. Cut off the excess fondant and use the cake paddle to smooth the cake even more. Tuck the edges in neatly under the cake. Proceed to cover the other two cakes. Leave overnight to harden.

Place a little Royal Icing (see page 113) on the cake stand before the bottom tier is placed on it to prevent the cake from sliding around. Cut four dowels the height of the bottom tier and insert in a square around the centre to support the second tier. Repeat for the third tier, but do not insert dowels into the top. Insert a dowel the height of the entire cake down the centre, through the holes in the dividers.

Fill the gaps between the tiers with Royal Icing. Brush the underside of each circle with confectioner's glue (see page 113) or Royal Icing and lightly press onto the cake.

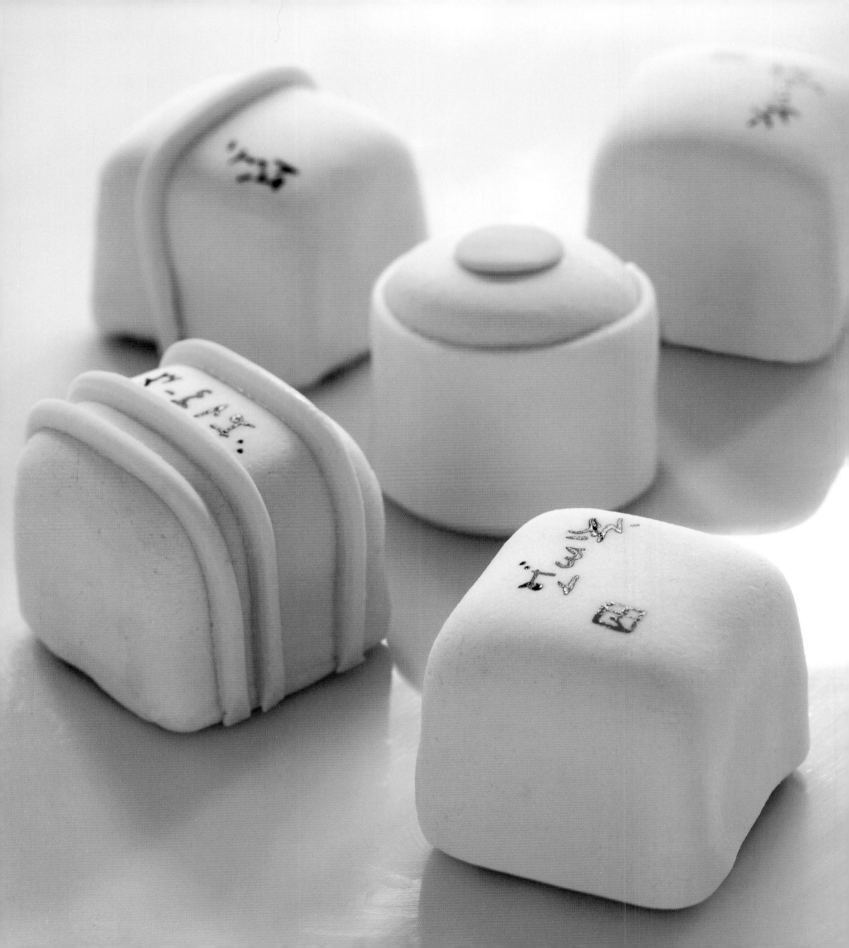

Petit Fours (Almond Cake)

This is one of our best-loved cakes, easily swaying those who never liked these versatile treats before (we call them Fancies in Cape Town). These little jewels can be decorated in such a huge variety of shapes and colours. The perfect wedding favour.

250 g butter
250 g marzipan, grated
3/4 cup (150 g) castor sugar
1/4 tsp (1.25 ml) almond essence
1/4 tsp (1.25 ml) vanilla essence
6 eggs, at room temperature
1 cup + 1 Tbsp (155 g) flour
2 tsp (10 ml) baking powder

Preheat the oven to 180 °C. Grease and line a 20-cm square pan. In the bowl of an electric mixer, with the paddle attachment, beat the butter and marzipan until creamy. Beat in the castor sugar, and both essences. Add the eggs, one at a time, scraping down the sides of the bowl regularly. Sift in the flour and baking powder and beat for 10 minutes. Pour the batter into the prepared pan and bake for 30 minutes, or until the centre of the cake springs back when lightly pressed. Cool completely in the pan. Cut into squares or rounds and cover the tops with a sheet of marzipan.
At Cakebread we use four methods for covering petit fours: Fondant (main photograph), Liquid Fondant, White Chocolate Icing and Royal Icing

WHITE CHOCOLATE ICING
300 g white chocolate, cut into pieces
1 1/5 cup (300 ml) cream
drop of edible colourant of choice

In a double boiler, melt the chocolate into the cream. Add a little food colouring. Cool until slightly thickened. Place the cake on a wire rack with a baking tray underneath. Pour the icing over the prepared cake, starting at the centre and moving out in a circular motion. Touch up the sides with a spatula.

LIQUID FONDANT
6 cups (840 g) icing sugar, sifted
1/2 cup (125 ml) water
1 Tbsp (15 ml) liquid glucose

In a large saucepan, over low heat, combine the icing sugar, water and glucose. Stir until slightly thickened but still pourable. Use in the same way as the White Chocolate Icing.

CHOCOLATE LIQUID FONDANT
6 cups (840 g) icing sugar, sifted
1/2 cup (125 ml) water
1 Tbsp (15 ml) liquid glucose
100 g chocolate, cut into pieces

In a large saucepan over low heat, combine the icing sugar, water, glucose and chocolate. Stir until slightly thickened but still pourable. Use in the same way as the White Chocolate Icing.

ROYAL ICING
4 egg whites
7 cups (1 kg) icing sugar, sifted
squeeze of lemon juice

In the bowl of an electric mixer, with the whisk attachment, lightly beat the egg whites while adding the icing sugar. The mixture should spread easily. Add the lemon juice. Beat on high for 10–15 minutes, or until the icing is light and pliable and retains its shape. Once well combined, check the consistency. If the sides of the bowl still look dry and crumbly, add some more egg white until the icing looks almost smooth but not wet.

Old~Fashioned

Da Island Cake

Go on, take a bite, close your eyes and think Caribbean island, blue skies, sunshine and yummy, cold, oversized cocktails!

1 cup (140 g) flour
2 tsp (10 ml) baking powder
pinch of salt
2 eggs, at room temperature
1 cup (200 g) sugar
1 tsp (5 ml) vanilla essence
1/2 cup (125 ml) milk
60 g butter
1 fresh pineapple
1 Tbsp (15 ml) sugar

PINEAPPLE ICING
4 egg yolks
1 1/2 cups (300 g) sugar
2 cups (500 ml) milk
pinch of salt
5 tsp (25 ml) cornflour
25 g butter
2 x 440 g cans crushed pineapple
2 cups (500 ml) cream
2 tsp (10 ml) pineapple essence
4 tsp (20 ml) castor sugar

Preheat the oven to 180 °C. Grease and line 2 x 18-cm cake pans. In a mixing bowl, sift the flour, baking powder and salt together. In another bowl, whisk the eggs and sugar until pale yellow. Add the flour mixture to the egg mixture, and then stir in the vanilla. In a small saucepan over medium heat, bring the milk and butter to the boil, then slowly add this to the batter, stirring gently. Pour into the prepared pans and bake for 25–30 minutes, or until the centre of the cake springs back when lightly pressed. Cool in the pan for 10 minutes before turning out.

Peel and slice the pineapple into rings. Dust with sugar. Heat a griddle pan and grill over high heat to form grill marks. Set aside. Assemble the cake by spreading a generous amount of pineapple icing between the layers and on top. (We like to be extra generous with the filling, but you can easily halve the recipe.) Decorate with grilled pineapple.

In a mixing bowl, mix the egg yolks, sugar, milk, salt and cornflour together. Transfer to a double boiler and whisk constantly until cooked and thickened. Remove from heat and stir in butter and crushed pineapple. Set aside to cool completely.

In a separate bowl, whisk the cream, pineapple essence and castor sugar until thick. Fold this mixture into the custard mixture.

Our Gran's Famous Orange Cake

In the small West Coast town where we grew up, a baker's worth was measured by the cakes submitted for judging at the annual agricultural show. This one was always a winner.

185 g butter
2 cups (280 g) self-raising flour
1 cup (200 g) sugar
½ cup (125 ml) milk
3 eggs, at room temperature
3 Tbsp (45 ml) orange juice
½ tsp (2.5 ml) orange zest
1 tsp (5 ml) baking powder
¼ tsp (1.25 ml) salt

Preheat the oven to 180 °C.
Grease and line 2 x 18-cm round cake pans.
Place all the ingredients into the bowl of an electric mixer, with the paddle attachment. Beat for 6–8 minutes until it forms a rather stiff dough. Divide the dough equally between the two pans and bake for 30–35 minutes, or until the centre of the cake springs back when lightly pressed. Let cool for 10 minutes before turning out. Cool completely before icing and decorating. Sandwich the layers with Orange Buttercream Icing. Top with the Smooth Icing and decorate with orange zest.

ORANGE BUTTERCREAM ICING
125 g butter, softened
1½ cups (210 g) icing sugar, sifted
2 Tbsp (30 ml) milk
1 drop of orange essence
zest of 1 orange

In the bowl of an electric mixer, with the paddle attachment, beat the butter until pale and creamy. Add the icing sugar and half the milk. Beat until combined. Add the orange essence and zest. If the mixture is too firm, add the rest of the milk and beat until desired consistency.

SMOOTH ICING TOPPING
2 cups (280 g) icing sugar, sifted
⅓ cup (80 ml) orange juice, no pulp
zest of 1 orange to decorate

Mix the icing sugar and orange juice together, and then pour over the cake.

Peppermint Chocolate Cupcakes

I worked for four years on a yacht belonging to a Turkish gentleman and, naturally, we spent a lot of time each year in that wonderful country. However, each time I saw something lovely and green in the window of a bakery or ice-cream shop, it turned out to be pistachio flavoured, and not my beloved mint. I had my mom post me South African sweets and chocolates containing mint and baked a little piece of home for myself and my husband. – Mari-Louis

2 cups (400 g) sugar
1³/₄ cups (245 g) flour, sifted
¹/₂ cup (60 g) cocoa powder
1¹/₂ tsp (7.5 ml) baking powder
1¹/₂ tsp (7.5 ml) bicarbonate of soda
1 tsp (5 ml) salt
2 eggs
1 cup (250 ml) milk
¹/₂ cup (125 ml) vegetable oil
2 tsp (10 ml) vanilla essence
1 cup (250 ml) boiling water
100 g mint chocolate, grated
mint sprigs to decorate

GANACHE
200 g dark chocolate, broken into small pieces
³/₄ cup (190 ml) cream
2 sprigs of mint, chopped

Place the chocolate pieces into a small metal bowl.

In a small saucepan, infuse the cream with the mint over low heat – do not bring to the boil. Strain and pour the cream over the chocolate. Leave for a few minutes, and then stir until the chocolate has melted. Cool slightly until thick enough to coat the cupcakes.

Preheat the oven to 180 °C. Line a muffin pan with 18 paper cups. Combine the dry ingredients in the bowl of an electric mixer, using a paddle attachment, then add the eggs, milk, oil and vanilla essence. Beat for 2 minutes on a medium speed. Stir in the boiling water until a thin batter has formed. Stir in the grated chocolate. Pour the batter into the paper cups and bake for 10–12 minutes. Remove from the oven and allow to cool before icing. Dip the cupcakes face down into the ganache. Decorate with fresh mint sprigs.

Crêpe Cake

A cake that really shows the Cakebread philosophy. Church Bazaar meets High Style meets the most important thing to all cakes … Taste!
This recipe make 40 medium pancakes.

4 cups (560 g) flour
1 tsp (5 ml) baking powder
2 tsp (10 ml) salt
4 cups (1 litre) milk
6–8 eggs, beaten
1 cup (250 ml) water
cinnamon-sugar
2 x quantities Pastry Cream (custard) (see page 78)
4 Tbsp (60 ml) castor sugar

Line a 23-cm spring form cake pan with baking paper.
In a mixing bowl, sift the flour, baking powder and salt together. Add a little of the milk. Stir until the mixture is smooth and without lumps. Gradually add the remaining milk. Add the eggs and beat well. Add some of the water if the batter isn't runny enough. Leave the mixture to rest for at least 3 hours.

Pour a little of the mixture into a hot, greased frying pan (Teflon-coated works best) and cook until pale brown on both sides. (The pan should be about the same diameter as the cake pan.) Sprinkle each pancake with cinnamon-sugar. Cool completely.

To assemble, place a pancake on the bottom of the spring form pan. Spread with pastry cream. Repeat until all the pancakes are stacked (do not spread pastry cream on the top of the stack). Refrigerate to set for 4–6 hours.

Sprinkle the top of the cake with the castor sugar, and then place under a hot grill to caramelize the top, or do it the easy way and use a blowtorch. This should not take longer than 2 minutes, as you do not want the custard to heat up again.

Loosen the sides of the spring form pan and unmould. Serve with a smile.

White Chocolate Mud Cake with Grape Medley

It may not be old-fashioned in our neck of the woods, but every New Zealander we've ever met has a favourite version of this dense cake. Pairing it with a grape medley is both an ode to our roots in a wine-producing valley and a way to make this our own.

250 g butter, diced

180 g white chocolate

1½ cups (300 g) sugar

¾ cup (190 ml) milk

1½ cups (210 g) flour

½ cup (70 g) self-raising flour

2 eggs, lightly beaten

1 tsp (5 ml) vanilla essence

Preheat the oven to 170 °C.

Grease and line a 23-cm round cake pan.

In a double boiler, melt the butter, white chocolate, sugar and milk over low heat. Stir continuously until the sugar dissolves. Transfer the mixture to a large mixing bowl, and then sift the flours into the bowl. Add the eggs and vanilla essence and stir to combine. Spoon the batter into the prepared cake pan and bake for 1 hour and 20 minutes. Cover the top with foil and return to the oven for another 20 minutes. Cool the cake in the pan.

Serve with the Grape Medley.

GRAPE MEDLEY

½ cup (100 g) sugar

¾ cup (190 ml) water

500 g grapes, different varieties

1 Tbsp (15 ml) rosemary leaves

¼ cup (65 ml) red wine

In a deep saucepan over medium to high heat, dissolve the sugar in the water, and then simmer until a caramel forms. Add the grapes carefully to prevent the hot caramel from spattering. Add the rosemary leaves and red wine. Stir until smooth. Strain and leave the grapes and caramel to cool separately.

To serve, top the white chocolate mud cake with grapes and rosemary, and then drizzle the wine caramel over the mud cake.

Pavlova Roulade

Reminds me of myself, all cracks and dilapidated glamour, but still oh so sweet and sexy. – Callie

7 egg whites	**TOPPING**
2 cups (400 g) castor sugar	2 cups (500 ml) whipping cream
1 Tbsp (15 ml) cornflour	2 Tbsp (30 ml) castor sugar
¹/₂ cup (60 g) hazelnuts, roughly chopped	1 tsp (5 ml) vanilla essence
	1 x 250 g punnet fresh raspberries
	2 Tbsp (30 ml) icing sugar

Preheat the oven to 200 °C. Grease and line a baking tray.

In the bowl of an electric mixer, with a whisk attachment, whisk the egg whites on high speed until stiff peaks form. Mix together the castor sugar and cornflour and then gradually add this to the egg whites in a gentle, steady stream. Keep whisking until all the sugar has been incorporated and the mixture is glossy and very stiff.

Using a spatula, spread the mixture onto the prepared tray and even out. Sprinkle with hazelnuts, and then bake for 10–12 minutes until golden in colour. Lower the heat to 160 °C and bake for another 15 minutes, or until firm to the touch. Remove from the oven and turn out onto a slightly damp kitchen towel, just like you would a swiss roll. Remove the baking paper from the back of the meringue and allow to cool for 10 minutes.

To make the topping, whisk the cream and castor sugar until firm. Add the vanilla essence and incorporate. Spread the cream evenly over the meringue and sprinkle with raspberries (reserve a few for decorating). Roll up the meringue from the long end, exactly like a swiss roll. (Don't fret if the meringue cracks while rolling, this is part of the beauty of the end product.)

Dust with the icing sugar and decorate with the reserved raspberries. Serve immediately.

Cherry Loaf

This tea-time loaf has been our mother's signature Christmas cake for years. If kept wrapped and stored in an airtight container, it will last for up to 2 weeks.

250 g butter, softened
1¼ cups (250 g) castor sugar
6 eggs, at room temperature
1 tsp (5 ml) vanilla essence
1¾ cups (245 g) flour
2 tsp (10 ml) baking powder
pinch of salt
3 Tbsp (45 ml) milk
½ cup (100 g) glazed red cherries
½ cup (60 g) mixed nuts of choice

Preheat the oven to 160 °C. Grease a large, 30-cm loaf pan.

In the bowl of an electric mixer, with the paddle attachment, cream the butter and castor sugar together. Add the eggs, one at a time, remembering to scrape down the sides regularly. Beat for 8 minutes. Add the vanilla essence. Sift the flour, baking powder and salt into the mixture. Add the milk and beat until well incorporated.

Stir the cherries into the mixture along with the nuts. Spoon into the prepared pan and bake for 1 hour, or until the centre of the cake is firm. (After 40 minutes, you can add more cherries and nuts to the top of the cake and push them in slightly.) Rest the cake for 10 minutes before turning out.

To fit in with the festive season you can also add chopped dried figs and glazed green cherries.

Mrs M's Texas Sheet Cake

Once more to the ocean and the lovely Mrs M. I used this recipe a lot when a bunch of unexpected guests dropped by. Delicious, rich, moist, enough-to-feed-a-crowd cake in 40 minutes, start to finish.

2 cups (280 g) flour
2 cups (400 g) sugar
250 g butter
4 Tbsp (60 ml) cocoa powder
1 cup (250 ml) water
1 cup (250 ml) milk
½ tsp (2.5 ml) white vinegar
2 eggs
1½ tsp (7.5 ml) ground cinnamon
1 tsp (5 ml) bicarbonate of soda
1 tsp (5 ml) vanilla essence

Preheat the oven to 180 °C. Grease a 23 x 32 cm rectangular pan. Sift the flour and sugar together. Set aside.
In a medium saucepan, bring the butter, cocoa powder and water to the boil. Pour this over the flour mixture and stir to combine. In a small mixing bowl, whisk the milk, vinegar and eggs together. Add to the cocoa batter. Stir in the cinnamon, bicarbonate of soda and vanilla essence. Pour the batter into the prepared pan and bake for 25–30 minutes, or until the centre of the cake springs back when lightly pressed. Leave to cool in the pan before turning out onto a wire rack.
Pour the Chocolate Glaze over the sheet cake.
Cut into squares and serve with cold milk.

CHOCOLATE GLAZE
110 g butter
4 Tbsp (60 ml) cocoa powder
6 Tbsp (90 ml) milk
1 cup (140 g) icing sugar, sifted
1 cup (120 g) coarsely chopped pecan nuts (hazelnuts or pistachios work just as well)

In a saucepan, heat the butter, cocoa powder and milk. Bring to a boil for 2–3 minutes until syrupy in consistency. Take off the heat and stir in the icing sugar and half of the nuts. Pour the glaze over the cake and decorate with the remaining nuts.

OPTION: Drizzle melted chocolate over the glaze to form patterns..

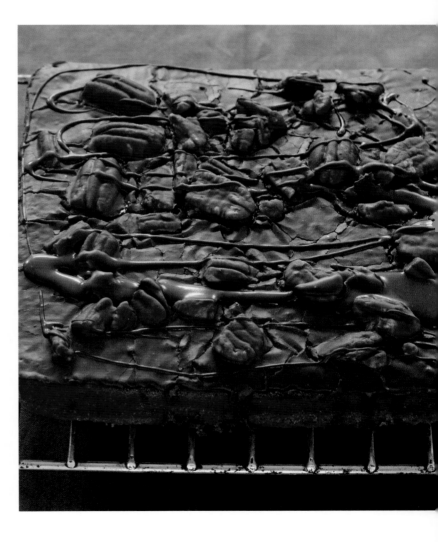

Poppy Seed Cake

Our grandfather's pride were the eight orange trees he kept in the garden and our first job upon visiting was to pick and collect the oranges that his back no longer allowed him to reach. We were then rewarded with big, lush oranges that he would peel with a pocket knife right there in his orchard. The result is a love of all things orange, like this colourful, flavourful garnish. The perfect topping.

6 eggs

1¼ cups (250 g) castor sugar

185 g butter, softened

1½ cups (150 g) ground almonds

1 cup (140 g) flour

2 Tbsp (30 ml) poppy seeds

2 tsp (10 ml) finely grated orange zest

FILLING/TOPPING

1 cup (250 g) cream cheese

150 g ricotta cheese

1½ cups (210 g) icing sugar

CANDIED ORANGE ZEST

2 oranges

⅓ cup (80 ml) water

1 cup (200 g) sugar

Wash the oranges, then trim away the zest. Remove and discard any pith stuck to the zest. Cut the zest into long, thin strips. Place in a small saucepan, cover with water and simmer for 5 minutes.

Drain, return to the pan with the ⅓ cup water and ⅓ cup (70 g) sugar and cook over low heat for 12–15 minutes.

Remove from the saucepan, separate the strips and allow to cool. Roll the strips in the remaining sugar until coated.

Preheat the oven to 180 °C. Grease a 20-cm square cake pan and line the bottom with baking paper.

In the bowl of an electric mixer, with the whisk attachment, whisk the eggs and castor sugar on high speed. Whisk in the butter. Into this batter, sift the almonds and flour. Add the poppy seeds and zest, and stir to combine.

Spoon the batter into the prepared pan, level the mixture and bake for 45–50 minutes, or until the centre of the cake springs back when lightly pressed. Let the cake cool in the pan, then turn out and cut the cake in half horizontally.

For the filling/topping: In the bowl of an electric mixer, with the paddle attachment, beat the cream cheese, ricotta and icing sugar until smooth. Spread half the filling over one layer of the cake, top with the next layer and spread with the remaining filling. Top all this with Candied Orange Zest and serve.

New Wave

Orange and Hazelnut Yoghurt Cake

Smells like heaven while baking and the combination of oranges and hazelnuts is wonderful. This recipe allows for many variations, so substitute the oranges with mandarins, blood oranges or tangerines, and use almonds instead of hazelnuts. In the photograph we used a variation of dried orange peel and candied oranges.

2¹/₂ cups (350 g) self-raising flour, sifted
1 cup (115 g) ground hazelnuts
³/₄ cup (150 g) castor sugar
1 tsp (5 ml) baking powder
2 large eggs, lightly beaten
1 cup (250 ml) Bulgarian yoghurt
¹/₂ cup + 2 Tbsp (155 ml) sunflower oil
zest of 1 lemon

Preheat the oven to 180 °C. Grease a Bundt pan. Place all the cake ingredients in a large mixing bowl, and beat until thoroughly mixed. Pour the batter into the prepared pan and bake for 30–45 minutes or until the centre of the cake springs back when lightly pressed. Pour three-quarters of the syrup over the hot cake as soon as it comes out of the oven. Let it cool. Reheat the remaining syrup until pourable again and brush the cake with the syrup for extra shine. Decorate with either Dried Orange Peel, Candied Orange Slices or Wedges, or a combination of these.

ORANGE SYRUP
1 cup + 2 Tbsp (280 ml) water
1³/₄ cups (350 g) castor sugar
juice of 1 orange
juice of 1 lemon
zest of 1 orange

While the cake is baking, combine all the syrup ingredients in a medium saucepan and gently bring to the boil, stirring until all the sugar has dissolved.

DRIED ORANGE PEEL
3 oranges

Peel the oranges, making sure there is hardly any pith remaining. Place the peel on a baking tray and dry in the oven at 110 °C for 15–20 minutes, or until the sides curl up.

QUICK CANDIED ORANGE SLICES
3 oranges
2 Tbsp (30 ml) castor sugar

Wash and slice the oranges into rounds. Line a baking tray with baking paper, and then sprinkle with 1 Tbsp (15 ml) of the castor sugar. Arrange the orange slices on the tray, and sprinkle with the rest of the sugar. Dry in the oven at 110 °C for about 30 minutes, or until the sides start curling up.

CANDIED ORANGE WEDGES
4 cups (800 g) sugar
2 cups (500 ml) water
3 oranges, cut into eighths, peel and all

In a small saucepan over medium heat, dissolve the sugar in the water. Add the oranges and simmer for 20 minutes until transparent. Remove the saucepan from the heat, but do not remove the contents. Leave overnight. Place in a sterilized jar and use as required.

Beetroot and Blueberry Cake

'The beet is the most intense of vegetables. The radish, admittedly, is more feverish, but the fire of the radish is a cold fire, the fire of discontent, not of passion. Tomatoes are lusty enough, yet there runs through tomatoes an undercurrent of frivolity. Beets are deadly serious.'
So Tom Robbins begins his novel, Jitterbug Perfume. *A book worth reading as much as this cake is worth baking.*

1 cup (250 g) beetroot, cooked and peeled (reserve the juice)
75 g dark chocolate, broken into pieces
125 g butter, softened
1¹/₂ cups (250 g) dark brown sugar
3 eggs
1¹/₂ cups (210 g) self-raising flour
3 Tbsp (45 ml) cocoa powder, sifted
1 tsp (5 ml) salt
1 cup (100 g) blueberries, smashed

Preheat the oven to 180 °C.
Grease and line 2 x 18-cm round cake pans.
Cut the beetroot into cubes and liquidize. Set aside.
In a double boiler, melt the chocolate with the butter. Set aside.
In the bowl of an electric mixer, with the paddle attachment, whisk the sugar and eggs together until ribbony. Sift the flour, cocoa powder and salt into this mixture. Stir in the liquidized beetroot and the blueberries.

Spoon the batter into the prepared pans, and then bake for 45 minutes, or until the centre of the cake springs back when lightly pressed. Pour the syrup over the cakes as soon as they come out of the oven (reserve up to 2 tsp (10 ml) syrup for the icing). Cool completely before turning out.
To assemble, trim the sides of the cakes to reveal the deep red hue. Spread the bottom layer with icing and top with the second layer. Ice the top of the cake with the remaining icing and decorate with fresh blueberries.

SYRUP
1 cup (250 ml) reserved beetroot juice
¹/₂ cup (125 ml) blueberry juice
¹/₂ cup (100 g) sugar

While the cake is baking, prepare the syrup. In a saucepan over medium heat, combine the beetroot juice and blueberry juice with the sugar, and stir until the sugar has dissolved. Simmer gently until it develops a syrupy consistency.

WHITE CHOCOLATE ICING
100 g white chocolate, broken into pieces
4 Tbsp (60 ml) cream
125 g butter, softened
2¹/₂ cups (500 g) icing sugar, sifted
¹/₂ tsp (2.5 ml) vanilla essence
dash of beetroot syrup

In a double boiler, melt the chocolate into the cream. Set aside and allow to cool down slightly.
In the bowl of an electric mixer, with a paddle attachment, cream the butter and icing sugar together. Add the vanilla essence. With the mixer on low speed, gradually add the chocolate mixture. With a wooden spoon, gently fold in the beetroot syrup to form swirls of colour; do not fully incorporate.

Eton Mess

'Mess' refers to the appearance of the topping for this cake, which has its origin at Eton College. The anecdotal story we like best is that a Labrador sitting on a picnic basket in the back of a car inadvertently created a new fad.

3 cups (420 g) flour
1½ tsp (7.5 ml) bicarbonate of soda
1½ tsp (7.5 ml) baking powder
¾ tsp (3.75 ml) salt

170 g butter, at room temperature
1½ cups (300 g) sugar
3 eggs
1 Tbsp (15 ml) vanilla essence
1½ cups (375 ml) buttermilk

Preheat the oven to 180 °C. Grease a large 24 x 32 cm sheet cake pan.

Into a medium bowl, sift the flour, bicarbonate of soda, baking powder and salt. Set aside.

In the bowl of an electric mixer, with the paddle attachment, beat the butter and sugar until creamy. Beat in the eggs, one at a time. Mix in the vanilla essence. Add the flour mixture and buttermilk alternately to the butter mixture, ending with the flour. Beat on high speed for 1 minute.

Pour the batter into the prepared pan, and then bake for 50–60 minutes. Rest for 10 minutes before turning out. Once cooled completely, spoon the mess all over the cake.

'MESS'
The volume of the mess is all up to you, so we are not going to give exact measurements here.
3 cups (450 g) strawberries, hulled and sliced
a dash of sugar
a dash of port
meringues, broken up
cream, softly whipped

Mash half of the strawberries with a little sugar and port, and fold in the broken meringues and softly whipped cream. Fold in the rest of the strawberries.

Chocolate Macaroon Cake

I've been baking this delicious cake with its rocky topping for school bake sales since I was 13. It always sold out. – Mari-Louis

2 cups (400 g) sugar
1³/₄ cups (245 g) flour
³/₄ cup (90 g) cocoa powder
1¹/₂ tsp (7.5 ml) baking powder
1¹/₂ tsp (7.5 ml) bicarbonate of soda
1 tsp (5 ml) salt
2 eggs, at room temperature
1 cup (250 ml) milk
¹/₂ cup (125 ml) vegetable oil
2 tsp (10 ml) vanilla essence
1 cup (250 ml) boiling water

Preheat the oven to 180 °C.
Grease and line a 23 x 30 cm baking pan.
Sift the sugar, flour, cocoa powder, baking powder, bicarbonate of soda and salt into the bowl of an electric mixer, with a paddle attachment. Add the eggs, milk, oil and vanilla essence. Beat for 2 minutes on medium speed. Stir in the boiling water. The batter should be runny.
Pour the batter into the prepared baking pan, and then bake for 40–45 minutes, or until the centre of the cake springs back when lightly pressed. Cool in the pan, and then turn out.
Spread the hot topping over the cake and let it set before cutting the cake into squares with a serrated knife.

CHOCOLATE MACAROON TOPPING
¹/₂ cup (60 g) cocoa powder
125 g butter
2 cups (400 g) sugar
¹/₂ cup (125 ml) milk
3 cups (300 g) oats
1 cup (100 g) desiccated coconut
¹/₂ tsp (2.5 ml) vanilla essence

In a medium saucepan over medium heat, combine the cocoa powder, butter, sugar and milk. Stir until the sugar has dissolved, and then bring to a boil. Boil for exactly 5 minutes. Remove from the heat and stir in the oats, coconut and vanilla essence.

Easy, Easy Cake with Figs, Mascarpone and Honey

Our mother came across this recipe on a yellowed magazine cut-out while moving house. It really is the easiest cake ever. We top it with 'Summer Love', our name for this mix of figs, mascarpone and honey that is reminiscent of exotic Istanbul.

200 g butter
1 cup (200 g) sugar
4 eggs
1½ cups (210 g) flour
1 Tbsp (15 ml) baking powder
pinch of salt
2 Tbsp (30 ml) icing sugar
2 x 230 g tubs mascarpone cheese
fresh figs for topping
honey for drizzling

Preheat the oven to 180 °C. Grease a medium bread loaf pan.

In a mixing bowl, cream the butter and sugar until pale in colour. Add the eggs, one at a time, beating thoroughly.

In a separate bowl, sift the flour, baking powder and salt together. Fold this into the egg mixture. Pour the batter into the prepared pan and bake for 30–40 minutes. Cool in the pan for 10 minutes before turning out.

In a medium bowl, stir the icing sugar into the mascarpone cheese. Spread this mixture over the cake. Peel and cut the figs in half and arrange on top of the mascarpone. Drizzle it all with honey. Note that mascarpone discolours with time, so decorate and serve immediately.

Plum Friands

Mari-Louis was given this recipe by an Australian friend and fellow crew member on a yacht. It has been a firm favourite ever since. If plums are not your thing, substitute with an equal quantity of cherries and lemon zest or rhubarb when in season.

6 ripe plums
$1/2$ cup (100 g) light brown sugar
$1^1/2$ cups (210 g) icing sugar
$1/2$ cup (70 g) flour
1 cup (115 g) ground almonds or almond flour
6 egg whites, at room temperature
170 g butter, melted and cooled
1 tsp (5 ml) vanilla essence

Preheat the oven to 200 °C. Grease a friand pan or a baking tray.

Remove the pips from the plums and chop roughly. In a medium saucepan over medium heat, combine the plums and brown sugar. Heat until the sugar has melted. Set aside.

In a mixing bowl, sift the icing sugar and flour together, and then mix in the ground almonds.

Lightly beat the egg whites with a fork, and then fold them into the flour mixture. Add the butter and vanilla essence and combine with the batter, stirring gently. Divide the mixture evenly between the friand holes or pour into the baking tray.

Drain the plums from the syrup and place a tablespoon of plums on top of each friand. Bake for 15–20 minutes. Cool in the pan, then turn out and dust with icing sugar. If baked in a tray, cut into fingers.

MAKES 12

Hazelnut Meringue Cake

A very elegant option for any tea party, christening or summer afternoon wedding. Don't be intimidated by the look of this one, it's a walk in the park to make.

1 cup (140 g) flour, sifted
2 tsp (10 ml) baking powder
pinch of salt
110 g butter, softened
1¹/₂ cups (300 g) castor sugar
4 eggs, separated
3 Tbsp (45 ml) vanilla essence
5 Tbsp (75 ml) milk
2 tsp (30 g) icing sugar
³/₄ cup (90 g) hazelnuts, chopped

STRAWBERRY CREAM
1 cup (250 ml) cream
2 Tbsp (30 ml) strawberry jam
1 cup (150 g) fresh strawberries, hulled and halved

In the bowl of an electric mixer, with the whisk attachment, whisk the cream until stiff peaks form. Add the jam and the strawberries. Whisk for a few seconds until the jam is well incorporated and the fruit slightly smashed.

Preheat the oven to 180 °C. Grease and line 2 x 20-cm round pans. In a medium bowl, sift together the flour, baking powder and salt. Set aside.
In the bowl of an electric mixer, with the paddle attachment, beat the butter and ¹/₂ cup (100 g) of castor sugar until pale and fluffy. Add the egg yolks and beat until combined. Turn mixer to low speed and gradually add the vanilla essence, the flour mixture and the milk. The batter should look smooth.
Divide the batter between the prepared pans. Set aside.
In the clean bowl of an electric mixer, with the whisk attachment, whisk the egg whites until thick and soft peaks form. With the mixer on medium speed, gradually whisk in the rest of the castor sugar and the icing sugar. Increase speed to high and whisk until stiff peak stage. Spread this meringue over the batter in the pans and sprinkle with hazelnuts.
Bake for 30–40 minutes. Cool cakes completely and carefully remove from pans. Sandwich the layers together with the Strawberry Cream.

Fudgy Chocolate Cake with Pistachio Crumbs

Cut a large chunk! Grab it and take a large bite! Leave teeth marks! Feel like a real man! – Callie

2¹/₂ cups (350 g) flour

1 Tbsp (15 ml) baking powder

2 cups (400 g) sugar

1 cup (120 g) cocoa powder, sifted

200 g unsalted butter, melted

3 large eggs

1 cup (250 ml) milk

¹/₂ cup (125 ml) vegetable oil

CHOCOLATE ICING

1¹/₄ cups (315 ml) cream

200 g milk chocolate, broken into pieces

1 tsp (5 ml) golden syrup

1 cup (200 g) shelled pistachios, chopped

Preheat the oven to 180 °C. Grease and line a 23-cm cake pan. Place all the ingredients in a large bowl and mix well to combine. Pour the mixture into the prepared pan and bake for about 1 hour. Rest for 5 minutes, turn out and cool completely. Ice the cake with Chocolate Icing and sprinkle with the pistachio nuts.

In a small saucepan, heat the cream to almost boiling point, and then pour it over the chocolate pieces in a large bowl. Leave for a few minutes, and then stir until the chocolate is smooth and glossy. Add the syrup. Cool completely.

Let's Celebrate

Hazelnut Gooey Brownies

The story goes that brownies (named after their colour) were born from a flop – someone forgot to add baking powder to a cake recipe and ended up with a flat but rather tasty treat. This fits in nicely with another of our philosophies: 'We don't make mistakes, we just constantly try to create new recipes.'

2¹/₂ cups (375 g) semi-sweet chocolate chips or
   chopped chocolate
250 g butter, softened
1 cup (200 g) sugar
4 large eggs
pinch of salt
³/₄ cup (105 g) flour
2 tsp (10 ml) vanilla essence
1 cup (120 g) coarsely chopped toasted hazelnuts

TOPPING
300 g semi-sweet chocolate, chopped
75 g white chocolate, chopped

Preheat the oven to 180 °C. Grease a 25 x 40 cm shallow baking pan.

In a double boiler, melt the chocolate with the butter. Remove from the heat and set aside.

In the bowl of an electric mixer, with the whisk attachment, beat the sugar and eggs until light and creamy. Stir in the salt, flour and vanilla essence. Add the chocolate mixture, and then stir in the nuts.

Spread the batter in the prepared pan and bake for about 30 minutes. The centre should still be soft and moist. Let it cool.

Melt the semi-sweet chocolate and pour and spread it over the cake. Melt the white chocolate and drizzle (using a fork) over the top to create patterns. Cut into squares.

MAKES ABOUT 12

Viennese Brownies

This is Callie's ultimate favourite which is equally at home at sophisticated events and children's parties. Serving it slightly heated makes it even more morish.

1 cup (250 g) cream cheese
½ cup (100 g) white sugar
3 eggs, at room temperature
1 tsp (5 ml) vanilla essence
300 g unsweetened chocolate, chopped
110 g butter, unsalted
1 cup (170 g) brown sugar
¾ cup (105 g) flour
1½ tsp (7.5 ml) baking powder
1½ tsp (7.5 ml) salt
icing sugar for dusting

Preheat the oven to 180 °C. Coat a baking tray with cooking spray. In the bowl of an electric mixer, with the paddle attachment, soften the cream cheese. Add the white sugar, 1 egg and the vanilla essence. Set aside.
In a double boiler, melt the chocolate and butter. Set aside to cool. In a medium bowl, beat the remaining 2 eggs lightly with a fork, and then add the brown sugar. Combine this with the melted chocolate mixture. Sift the flour, baking powder and salt into the chocolate mixture and stir to combine.
Pour half of the chocolate batter into the prepared tray. Spread with the cream cheese mixture, and then top with the remaining batter. Bake for 45 minutes. Dust with icing sugar (follow our example to create clean lines), and then cut into blocks measuring 5 x 5 cm.

MAKES ABOUT 35

TIPS: You can melt chocolate and butter in a microwave at a medium-high setting for 30 seconds.
Add hazelnuts to the chocolate batter for a different combination.

Madeleines

'She sent out for one of those short, plump little cakes called "petite madeleines", which look as though they had been moulded in the fluted scallop of a pilgrim's shell … an exquisite pleasure had invaded my senses…' Marcel Proust in Remembrance of Things Past: Swann's Way. *By no means a traditional Madeleine, but we feel Proust would approve of our buttery version.*

2 cups (280 g) flour
1¼ cups (250 g) sugar
1 Tbsp (15 ml) baking powder
½ tsp (2.5 ml) salt
110 g butter, melted
2 eggs, lightly beaten with a fork
1 cup (250 ml) milk
1 tsp (5 ml) vanilla essence or seeds from 1 vanilla bean

Preheat the oven to 180 °C. Grease 2 Madeleine pans.
In a mixing bowl, sift the flour, sugar, baking powder and salt together. Add the melted butter, eggs, milk and vanilla essence. Mix until combined.
Spoon the batter into the prepared Madeleine pans, and then bake for 10–15 minutes. Turn out, wrap in napkins and serve hot with Raspberry and Cream Swirls.

RASPBERRY AND CREAM SWIRLS
2 cups (300 g) frozen raspberries
½ cup (100 g) sugar
½ cup (125 ml) cream, whipped

In a saucepan over medium heat, heat the berries and sugar until the sugar has dissolved. Bring to a boil, then reduce heat until shiny and thick. Cool slightly.
On a side plate, place a dollop of cream and a serving of raspberry sauce, forming a swirling pattern with a chopstick. Mop up with the hot Madeleines.

MAKES 24

Éclairs

Choux pastry dates back to the sixteenth century when it was apparently first baked for Catherine De Medici. We use the same recipe for all our éclairs, be they elegant French éclairs or small puffs for a croquembouche. While there are many variations on this traditional wedding dessert, the original features éclairs filled with pastry cream, dipped into hot caramel and then stacked into a tower. The name literally means 'crack in the mouth' and we are told that the groom would hack at the top of the tower with a sword, while bridesmaids would hold up the tablecloth and thus catch the crackly pieces before serving them to the guests.

125 g butter
³/₅ cup (150 ml) water
1 cup (140 g) flour, sifted
¹/₂ tsp (2.5 ml) salt
4 eggs, at room temperature
1 x quantity Pastry Cream (custard) (see page 78)

Preheat the oven to 200 °C.

Line a baking tray with baking paper or use a Silpad.

In a medium saucepan, melt the butter in the water, and then bring to the boil. Remove from the heat and add the flour and salt. Return the saucepan to the heat and stir very quickly until a ball forms and the dough comes away from the sides. Transfer the dough to the bowl of an eletric mixer, with a paddle attachment; cool for 3 minutes. With the mixer on slow speed, add the eggs, one at a time, making sure each egg is fully incorporated before the next one is added. Beat until the dough is stiff and glossy. Use immediately.

Pipe the dough into whichever shape you desire. Make sure you don't pipe them too close together, as they do expand a fair bit. Bake regular size for 10 minutes, reduce the heat to 180 °C and bake for a further 15 minutes. (For smaller ones, bake for 7 minutes at each temperature setting.) Cool. You can now cut open the éclairs and fill with pastry cream (you can flavour this with coffee) or you could do a little baking trick and make a hole in the bottom of each éclair with the nozzle of your pastry bag and fill with cream through the hole. Dip into melted chocolate or make a shiny éclair glaze.

If pressed for time, simply mix a little icing sugar with lemon juice until pouring consistency, and pour over the éclairs. Unfilled, these éclairs freeze really well.

MAKES 24 SMALL OR 12 LARGE

Lamingtons

We fight over these like the Scots, Kiwis and Aussies fight over the rights to claim these as their own invention. Lord Lamington, whom the Australians claim they were named after, could not stomach these treats, calling them 'those bloody poofy woolly biscuits'. Use any sponge or sheet cake, cut into squares, dip into one of the chocolate mixtures below and roll in desiccated coconut.

WHITE CHOCOLATE

2 cups (270 g) white chocolate pieces

1 cup (250 ml) cream

1 Tbsp (15 ml) milk

2 cups (200 g) desiccated coconut

In a double boiler, melt the chocolate and cream over low heat; stir until combined. Remove from the heat and beat until light and thick. Add the milk. Dip the lamingtons in the chocolate mixture, and then roll in the coconut.

DARK CHOCOLATE

¼ cup (30 g) cocoa powder

25 g butter

¼ cup (65 ml) milk

2 cups (280 g) icing sugar, sifted

2 cups (200 g) desiccated coconut

In a saucepan over medium heat, combine the cocoa powder, butter and milk. Stir until the butter has melted. Take off the heat and stir in the icing sugar. Dip the lamingtons in the chocolate mixture, and then roll in the coconut.

STRAWBERRY CHOCOLATE

2 cups (270 g) white chocolate pieces

1 cup (250 ml) cream

1 Tbsp (15 ml) milk

dash of strawberry essence

drop of red food colouring

2 cups (200 g) desiccated coconut

In a double boiler, melt the chocolate and cream over low heat; stir until combined. Remove from the heat and add the milk, essence and colouring. Dip the lamingtons in the chocolate mixture, and then roll in the coconut.

SERVING SUGGESTION: We like to stack all three colours together to resemble that favourite from our youth, Neapolitan ice cream.

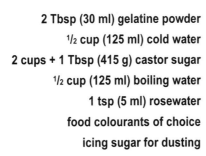

Marshmallows

Miles of smiles and pink fluffy clouds.

2 Tbsp (30 ml) gelatine powder
½ cup (125 ml) cold water
2 cups + 1 Tbsp (415 g) castor sugar
½ cup (125 ml) boiling water
1 tsp (5 ml) rosewater
food colourants of choice
icing sugar for dusting

Spray 2 baking pans with non-stick spray.

In the mixing bowl of an electric mixer, soak the gelatine in the cold water.

Set the mixing bowl over a double boiler, and allow the gelatine to melt. Remove from the heat. Add the castor sugar and boiling water. Attach the bowl to the mixer. Using the whisk attachment, beat on high speed for 8–10 minutes until the mixture is thick and shiny. Add the rosewater and stir through.

Divide the mixture into two parts and add to each the colourant of choice. Mix well and then pour the mixture into the prepared pans to a depth of about 1.5 cm. Refrigerate before cutting into desired shapes and dusting with icing sugar.

CAKEBREAD METHOD: We make all colours, flavouring green with apple essence, orange with orange, and yellow with pineapple or lemon essence.

For a traditional tasting marshmallow, keep pure white and add vanilla essence instead of rosewater.

MAKES 50 HEART SHAPES

Coconut Ice

Loved since we were kids.

2 cups (400 g) sugar
pinch of salt
1/2 cup (125 ml) water
1 Tbsp (15 ml) liquid glucose
1/4 tsp (1.25 ml) cream of tartar
2 cups (200 g) desiccated coconut
1 tsp (5 ml) vanilla essence
1 tsp (5 ml) rosewater
red food colouring

Grease a small sheet pan.
In a saucepan over medium heat, combine the sugar, salt, water, glucose and cream of tartar. Stir until the sugar has dissolved, then boil the mixture until it forms a soft ball when tested in cold water (115 °C when using a sugar thermometer). Using a fine brush, brush down the crystals that form on the sides of the pan. Remove from the heat and cool slightly.
Divide the mixture into two and set one half aside.
Add 1 cup of the coconut to the other half (this half will remain white). Add the vanilla essence. In the bowl of an electric mixer, with the paddle attachment, beat this white mixture until thick and creamy. Pour into the prepared pan.
Add the remaining coconut to what will become the pink part (the reserved half). Add the rosewater and food colouring. Beat until thick and creamy. Pour over the white mixture. Leave to set, and then cut into rectangles while still slightly soft.

TIP: We like to chop our coconut finer with a food processor to give a smoother finish.

Nougat

Probably our best loved treat at Cakebread, loaded with nuts and all sorts of interesting goodies. We occasionally add Turkish delight and also preserved figs. We are huge fans of rice paper; we wrap petit fours in it and even make a beautiful feathered wedding cake from it. Rice paper is a very fine, edible paper made from the pith of an Oriental tree. It is also helpful when baking meringues and macarons to protect the bottoms from burning or sticking.

2 sheets rice paper (15.5 x 23.5 cm)
2 cups (400 g) sugar
1 cup (250 ml) liquid glucose
¹/₂ cup (125 ml) golden syrup
2 egg whites
75 g butter, softened
1 tsp (5 ml) vanilla essence
1 cup (200 g) glazed red cherries
¹/₂ cup (100 g) glazed green cherries
¹/₂ cup (60 g) chopped pecans or walnuts

Grease a 15 x 22 cm rectangular pan and line with one sheet of rice paper.

In a medium saucepan over low heat, combine the sugar, glucose and golden syrup. Stir until the sugar has dissolved. Turn up the heat and, without stirring, boil for 6 minutes (when using a sugar thermometer, it should read 138 °C – small crack stage). You can also test it by dropping a little of the sugar mixture into ice water; it will harden straight away. Remove the mixture from the heat.

In the bowl of an electric mixer, with a whisk attachment, whisk the egg whites until stiff peak stage. In a slow, thin stream, add the hot syrup and beat for 4 minutes, or until the mixture is very thick, shiny and holds its shape. Add the butter and vanilla essence and beat until thoroughly mixed. Stir in the cherries and nuts. Pour and spread the mixture into the prepared pan, and then cover with the second sheet of rice paper. Cool until set – 6–8 hours.

Turn the nougat out of the pan and, using cooking spray on your knife, cut into squares.

MAKES 15 SQUARES

Macarons

Rows and rows of these astoundingly jewel-like treats adorn every bakery in France. While beautiful in the original pastels, we like to be boldly daring with ours and attempt unusual colours like aubergine and shocking pink to match modern weddings.

100 g finely ground almonds (see Hint)
110 g icing sugar
2 egg whites
¹/₃ cup (70 g) castor sugar
pink and green food colouring
raspberry jam
whipped cream
berries

Preheat the oven to 130 °C. Line a baking tray with baking paper or a Silpad (preferred).
In a medium mixing bowl, sift the almond flour and icing sugar three times.
In the bowl of an electric mixer, with the whisk attachment, whisk the egg whites until stiff peaks form. Add the castor sugar spoon for spoon while continuously whisking, remembering to scrape down the sides of the bowl regularly. Whisk until the mixture becomes thick and shiny. Fold this mixture into the flour mixture. Stir in food colouring of choice until desired hue is achieved.
Pipe rounds (about 2.5 cm) onto the prepared tray, allowing plenty of space between each round. Bake for 15 minutes.
Open the oven door – leave the oven on – for another 20 minutes.
Switch off the oven, close the door, and leave the macarons to dry – 30 minutes.
Carefully lift the macarons off the baking paper with a flat knife. Stick two rounds together with jam or leave open and decorate with fresh cream and berries.

MAKES 30 (OR 15 SANDWICHES)

HINT: Start with 200 g of finely ground almonds and sift until you end up with 100 g very fine almond flour.
At Cakebread we sometimes add a drop of almond essence to enhance the flavour of our *macarons*.

Pastel Meringues

Meringues are a baker's dream. Delicious and shiny as an icing, or baked into any shape, size or colour …

4 large egg whites
1 cup (200 g) castor sugar
pink, yellow and green food colouring

Preheat the oven to 140 °C. Line 2 baking trays with Silpads or baking paper.

In the bowl of an electric mixer, with a whisk attachment, whisk the egg whites until soft peak stage. Gradually add the castor sugar, one tablespoon at a time, making sure to incorporate completely. Whisk until stiff peak stage and very shiny.

Keep white or colour with drops of food colouring. Pipe desired shapes onto the prepared tray or do it free form with the back of a spoon. Bake for 1 hour, and then switch off the stove and let the meringues dry and cool in the oven.

BAKER'S SECRET: To get the mottled effect of our meringues, lightly dust them with edible coloured powder before baking.

Fortune Cookies

This is one of those quirky bride requests that sounded far-fetched at the time, but has now become one of our staples at Cakebread. We make them in all sorts of colours and seal them in cellophane. They really do make the most fun wedding favour.

¹/₂ **cup (70 g) flour**
1¹/₂ **tsp (7.5 ml) cornflour**
¹/₄ **tsp (1.25 ml) salt**
¹/₂ **cup (100 g) sugar**
1 **Tbsp (15 ml) water**
2 **egg whites**
¹/₂ **tsp (2.5 ml) vanilla essence**
¹/₂ **tsp (2.5 ml) almond essence**
3 **Tbsp (45 ml) vegetable oil**
red food colouring

We use 2 pans as you can fold a few while waiting for others to bake. Limit batches to 2–3 per pan, as the cookies harden quickly and you will not have enough time to fold more than this number.

MAKES 12–15

The first step is to type silly messages and predictions and cut them into small strips of paper (no longer than 8 cm). Preheat the oven to 180 °C. Grease 2 large baking trays or use a Silpad (preferred).
In a mixing bowl, sift the flour, cornflour, salt and sugar together. Stir the water into the flour mixture.
In a medium bowl, lightly beat the egg whites, vanilla and almond essences and oil together. Using a hand whisk, whisk until frothy. Add the flour mixture to the egg mixture and stir until you have a smooth batter. The batter is slightly runny, but when you pour it, it keeps its shape. Add a drop of food colouring – be careful here, a little goes a long way.
We use acetate sheets (from art shops) with cut-outs to keep all the cookies the same size. We use a 10-cm cut-out. Layer the acetate sheets over the prepared baking trays (we find a Silpad works wonders here). Spread a thin layer of batter over the holes in the acetate, then clean the sides. Bake for 10 minutes or until the sides start to curl.
Take out of the oven, place a message on the inside and, working quickly, fold the cookie in half and then bring the points together. A glove will help as this is rather hot work.

Old~Fashioned Waffles (using a Waffle Iron)

Our lovely Aunt Annelie's recipe, handed down to her from her Aunt Gesela, handed down to her from her Aunt ... you get the message. Pure nostalgia. Scratch around in old markets to find these very cool waffle irons.

2 eggs
1 cup (140 g) flour
1 tsp (5 ml) sugar
1 tsp (5 ml) baking powder
pinch of salt
1 cup (250 ml) water
3 cups (750 ml) vegetable oil

In a glass bowl, lightly beat the eggs. Into these, sift the flour, sugar, baking powder and salt. Add the water. Stir until well combined.

In a medium saucepan, heat the oil until medium hot. Place the iron into the oil until well heated. Remove from the heat, dip into the batter and then back into the hot oil. Cook until light brown – the waffles should pop off on their own. If not, remove with the point of a knife. Serve with honey or syrup of choice.

MAKES ABOUT 20

Jordan Almonds

We'd never considered making these until a bride requested some in unusual colours. They turned out to be loads of fun when we started playing around with different hues and combinations.

4 egg whites, at room temperature
1 cup (200 g) sugar
pinch of salt
drop of food colouring of choice
100 g whole almonds
100 toothpicks

In the heatproof bowl of an electric mixer, combine the egg whites, sugar and salt. Set over a pan of simmering water. Whisk continuously for 3–5 minutes until the sugar has dissolved and the mixture is hot to the touch.

Attach the bowl to the electric mixer and, using the whisk attachment, beat on high speed for 7 minutes until the mixture has cooled down and stiff peaks form. Swirl in a drop of colouring – do not mix through.

Skewer the almonds with the toothpicks. Dip each almond into the mixture until well coated, then set aside to dry overnight (we push them into a foamalite board). Remove the toothpicks only when dried. While delicious, these never harden quite as much as the store-bought version.

Sugar Cookies

Delicious, easy and versatile. We turn these easy cookies into all kinds of fun shapes.

200 g butter, softened
1 cup (200 g) castor sugar
1 egg, lightly beaten
3 cups (420 g) flour
1 tsp (5 ml) vanilla essence

Preheat the oven to 200 °C. Grease a baking tray.

In the bowl of an electric mixer, with the paddle attachment, cream the butter and castor sugar. Add the egg, flour and vanilla essence. Mix until combined.

Shape the dough into a ball, wrap in plastic and refrigerate for 1 hour before using.

Dust the work surface with flour and roll out the cookie dough to the preferred thickness. Cut into shapes. Place the cookies on the prepared tray, leaving some space between each one. Refrigerate for another 30 minutes.

Bake the cookies for 8–10 minutes, or until golden brown. Decorate with rolled fondant or pipe and flood them with Royal Icing, as in our example.

ROYAL ICING
2 egg whites
2¹/₂ cups (350 g) icing sugar, sifted
juice of ¹/₂ lemon

In the bowl of an electric mixer, with the paddle attachment, beat the egg whites, icing sugar and lemon juice together. Start on low speed and increase speed as the mixture gets smoother. If the mixture is too dry, add more egg white.

You need to have a soft-peak consistency for piping. For filling in spaces, add a few drops of water to make the icing more runny. Always keep your icing covered with clingfilm to prevent it from drying out.

Crispy Rice Squares

The popular name for these treats is trademarked so we will use a generic name instead. Three simple ingredients in three easy steps. Also fun to play around with other puffed grain cereals using the same recipe.

45 g butter
250 g marshmallows
6 cups Rice Krispies®

Line a 20 x 25 cm sheet pan with baking paper. Grease the sides.

In a saucepan over medium heat, melt the butter. Stir in the marshmallows until they start melting, and then stir in the Rice Krispies until well combined.

Spoon the mixture into the pan and level. Cool before turning out and cutting into squares.

OPTIONAL: Drizzle with melted white chocolate.

Sugar Lollies

Just so absolutely gorgeous and mouthwatering. We've never seen a child walk past them without wanting one. We introduced some gold leaf to ours to show that grown-ups can have fun too.

4 cups (800 g) sugar
1 cup (250 ml) water
¼ tsp (1.25 ml) cream of tartar
drop of food colouring of choice

You will need a lolly mould and lolly sticks. Pour the sugar into a saucepan, and then add the water and cream of tartar – do not stir. Set over medium heat. When the sugar has dissolved, add the food colouring, and then allow to boil until hard crack stage (test this by dropping a little of the syrup into a glass of cold water – if it sets right away, it is ready). Carefully (it is very hot) pour the syrup into the moulds and position the lolly sticks. Cool for 30 minutes before unmoulding.

Index of Recipes